LEADERS WHO FOLLOW

ANDY MASON

10 Publishing
a division of 10 of those.com

First published in Great Britain in 2022

British Library Cataloguing in Publication Data
A record for this book is available from the British Library

ISBN: 978-1-914966-68-2

Designed by Jude May
Cover image © ikril, detshana | Adobe Stock

Printed in Denmark by Nørhaven

Evangelical Press (EP Books), an imprint of 10Publishing
Unit C, Tomlinson Road, Leyland, PR25 2DY, England
Email: info@10ofthose.com
Website: www.10ofthose.com

1 3 5 7 10 8 6 4 2

Acknowledgments

This book was written during a time of study leave, so I'm very thankful to our church council for setting me free from normal duties to focus on it. I'm also, as always, so grateful to Kathrine, my wife, for her patience in supporting me writing this. I hope that one day our kids, Ori and Pella, might read this. Whether or not they are ever spiritual leaders of some kind, I hope they might think that their dad, sinner as he was, tried to live this out and that they will be spurred on to know King Jesus better.

Contents

Introduction

> So they pulled their boats up on shore, left everything and *follow*ed him (Luke 5:11, my emphasis).

This is a book all about how to follow Jesus in Christian ministry. In my previous book, *God's Leader*, I focused on a wide number of different biblical passages and applied them to ministry. There I explored a whole range of issues connected to spiritual leadership. This book has a narrower focus: it centres on the relationship between spiritual leaders and the Lord Jesus. All the Gospels present the command 'follow me' as the starting point for discipleship and ministry (Matt. 4:19; Mark 1:17; Luke 5:27; John 1:43). We are followers before we ever lead others, and that following is key to everything that we do. We lead out of following.

We mustn't miss, though, that the real issue at hand isn't simply our following, but the Person we are following. When Jesus says 'follow me', the 'me' refers to the infinite, glorious, loving Alpha and Omega of the universe. He is the One who defines us and shapes us in life and ministry.

Life and leadership is all about him. Thus, our relationship with Jesus has to be the clear starting point for all we do. Without him, we have nothing to say and nothing to offer to the world. Jesus is the heart of all ministry.

That said, it is also true that our walk with the Lord Jesus can easily be neglected as we become distracted and diverted in our spiritual responsibilities. Our leading can subsume our following, and we can become neglectful of the very One who brings us life. Such neglect, though easy to drift into, will always lead to dramatic and tragic consequences for both the leader and those he or she leads. This book is written to help us fight that neglect. I've tried to write a book that would strengthen me in my ministry, therefore much of it arises out of my own heart struggles, as well as addressing the heart struggles of other leaders I know. My goal is to strengthen our following of Jesus and to ensure that it is at the heart of our ministry. I want to keep calling us back to the One who our ministry is all about.

In *God's Leader*, I followed an expository method in looking at spiritual leadership, and I do the same here. So, again, this book isn't a systematic approach to spiritual leadership, but is focused on a number of texts from the Gospels of Luke and John. Systematic and expository methods both have their strengths and weaknesses, but it seems to me that much that is written on leadership is only systematic, and so getting our noses into specific texts is a really healthy thing to do. The simple meditation on God's word in the middle of ministry is very powerful and sustaining. As we do this, we meet Jesus afresh and directly experience his presence. This is how we commune with the One we are following. I hope the approach of this book will enable that.

I have consciously used Luke (one of the three synoptic Gospels that share many similarities) as well as John's Gospel so as to give a rounded flavour of all that it means to know and follow Jesus. However, this book doesn't aim to say everything about what it means to follow Jesus, nor everything about ministry. There are plenty of other passages that could be included, but hopefully major themes have been covered properly. The book can easily be used as part of daily devotions, read together in staff teams or simply read through as any other book. My hope is simply that we get a better view of Jesus and what it means to know him.

– 1 –

Following Jesus

One day as Jesus was standing by the Lake of Gennesaret, the people were crowding round him and listening to the word of God. He saw at the water's edge two boats, left there by the fishermen, who were washing their nets. He got into one of the boats, the one belonging to Simon, and asked him to put out a little from the shore. Then he sat down and taught the people from the boat.

When he had finished speaking, he said to Simon, 'Put out into deep water, and let down the nets for a catch.'

Simon answered, 'Master, we've worked hard all night and haven't caught anything. But because you say so, I will let down the nets.'

When they had done so, they caught such a large number of fish that their nets began to

> break. So they signalled to their partners in the other boat to come and help them, and they came and filled both boats so full that they began to sink.
>
> When Simon Peter saw this, he fell at Jesus' knees and said, 'Go away from me, Lord; I am a sinful man!' For he and all his companions were astonished at the catch of fish they had taken, and so were James and John, the sons of Zebedee, Simon's partners.
>
> Then Jesus said to Simon, 'Don't be afraid; from now on you will fish for people.' So they pulled their boats up on shore, left everything and followed him (Luke 5:1–11).

True spiritual leadership doesn't start with leading, but with following. We have to follow Jesus before we can ever lead for Jesus. If we have any authority, influence or power, it is all derived from the Lord, and not inherent to us. Accordingly, every leader must continually return to Jesus, as a living, nourishing relationship with him is the foundation for all that we do.

Surprised by the power of Jesus

Thankfully, Scripture has given us a great example of a leader who has, in the midst of weakness and sins, lived out a life of following Jesus: Peter. His story is a demonstration of the power and grace of Jesus Christ to transform and raise up an unlikely man to be a spiritual leader. In Luke 5:1–11, we meet Peter the fisherman, rather than Peter the apostle. As the story starts, we see that he has been out doing his job all night, but rather unsuccessfully. Through meeting Jesus, though, his life is about to be turned upside down and inside out. Jesus approaches Peter, gets into his boat and performs an amazing miracle. Beforehand, Peter's fishing had resulted only in empty nets. Now, through the power of Jesus, the nets become completely overloaded with wriggling fish. The shock is palpable.

Yet, while the catch is striking, it's not the most spectacular of Jesus' signs and wonders. After all, if Jesus really wanted to get attention, he could have done something much more breathtaking – such as parting the Sea of Galilee and walking through it! Further, in comparison with Jesus' other miracles, it isn't obviously altruistic. In other words, it's not a healing, a raising of the dead or an exorcism. So, while striking, it is in many ways also strange and inconsequential. We might ask ourselves, 'What's the point of this miracle?'

It seems that this sign is best understood as a personalised miracle for Simon. Fishing is, obviously, not a hobby for Peter, but his livelihood, and this is, by any standard, a dream catch for him. The irony with the miracle is that Peter, an experienced fisherman who knows the local waters, had caught nothing that day. Jesus, on the other hand, proves himself to be the best fisherman in Galilee for a hundred years – and without even having a fishing rod or getting himself wet! Jesus is clearly getting Simon's attention here. He's showing Simon (and us) that he is the One who gives, or withdraws, ultimate success. It's all in his hands.

As a result, this changes our perspective on everything that we do in life or ministry. The reality is that while we can do everything that we might think of, using all our powers and gifts, and working all day and night, we might yet still come up with nothing. We need to know that our greatest effort to build our churches, our greatest dreams for ministry and our every success are all under the authority of Jesus. Our 'fishing' is submitted to his purpose and plan, and the filling of our nets is controlled by him. He's Lord over everything, and dwarves all our efforts and hard work. The Lord Jesus can choose to give us our dreams with a snap of his fingers, or withhold if that is best. Maybe he'll bless us with everything we desire, or maybe he won't, but the truth is that he decides.

Humbled before Jesus

We know that Peter respected Jesus before the miracle. After all, Jesus had already healed his mother-in-law (4:38–39), and Peter calls Jesus 'Master' (5:5) and follows Jesus' directions about his boat! Yet now, through this miracle, Peter is granted a whole new insight into who Jesus is, and it completely changes his life. Peter's words say it all: 'Go away from me, Lord; I am a sinful man!' (v. 8).

It doesn't seem that Peter is confessing a particular kind of sin here, but rather that he is recognising Jesus' identity. In 4:34, an unclean spirit who Jesus is exorcising cries out in terror,'Go away! What do you want with us, Jesus of Nazareth? Have you come to destroy us? I know who you are – the Holy One of God!' There is a striking echo of these words in Peter. Of course, unlike the spirit, Peter isn't fighting Jesus here, but he does fall before him in self-humiliation. The sign of the full net has pointed him to the ultimate power, glory and holiness of Jesus. He understands that he's in the presence of the Holy One.

Yet, the really striking thing in this story is what has led Peter into this confession. Notice that it isn't a rebuke from Jesus. There's no indication in the passage that Jesus has told him off, or confronted him about sin in his life. On the contrary, Peter's eyes have been opened by the generous power of Jesus through this sign. The Lord has shown him his goodness in this miracle, and it's that very goodness that has convicted Peter of his unworthiness. We might wonder how goodness could be so convicting, but one of C. S. Lewis's science fiction trilogy helps explain the power of infinite goodness. In this scene, the main character finds himself before a kind of angelic presence. The passage is remarkable for the way it describes what it's like to encounter true goodness:

> My fear was now of another kind. I felt sure that the creature was what we call 'good', but I wasn't sure whether I liked 'goodness' so much as I had supposed. This is a very terrible experience. As long as what you are afraid of

> is something evil, you may still hope that the good may come to your rescue. But suppose you struggle through to the good and find that it also is dreadful? How if food itself turns out to be the very thing you can't eat, and home the very place you can't live, and your very comforter the person who makes you uncomfortable? Then, indeed, there is no rescue possible: the last card has been played. For a second or two I was nearly in that condition. Here at last was a bit of that world from beyond the world, which I had always supposed that I loved and desired, breaking through and appearing to my senses: and I didn't like it, I wanted it to go away. I wanted every possible distance, gulf, curtain, blanket and barrier to be placed between it and me.[1]

Peter has met the Lord and he's simply awestruck. Here we have a man who will become the great leader of the apostles, the preacher at Pentecost and a great miracle worker, but his starting point with Jesus is: 'Go away from me, Lord; I am a sinful man!' When did we last tremble before the wonderful love and goodness of the Lord Jesus? We too need our eyes opened once again to see his awe-inspiring generosity.

Appointed by Jesus

Peter finds himself overwhelmed and tells Jesus to leave him, but Jesus doesn't accede to Peter's request. He simply tells Peter not to be afraid (5:10). Of course, you only say that to someone if there is something that is potentially scary or threatening. When Jesus says this, he's not denying that he is almighty, holy and full of glory (all potentially scary things, as we've already seen!). Rather, he is declaring, 'I'm good and my intentions towards you are good.' Jesus has come to call Peter and appoint him to reach a lost world. Peter has just told Jesus to leave him, but now Peter is going to leave everything in order to follow Jesus (v. 11). Jesus' miraculous catch of fish will lead to Peter getting a whole new set of 'fishing skills' as he has his life turned upside down.

We have been summoned into ministry by an awesome and authoritative Lord. We tremble before him, but should not be afraid because he's wonderfully kind and good. Jesus has called us to leave civilian affairs behind (cf. 2 Tim. 2:4), and to give our lives to his service. Our purpose and goal is no longer set by our own predilections, but by his kingdom agenda. We now follow him.

Disowning Jesus

> 'Simon, Simon, Satan has asked to sift all of you as wheat. But I [Jesus] have prayed for you, Simon, that your faith may not fail. And when you have turned back, strengthen your brothers.'
>
> But he replied, 'Lord, I am ready to go with you to prison and to death.'

> Jesus answered, 'I tell you, Peter, before the cock crows today, you will deny three times that you know me' (Luke 22:31–34).

The call of Peter in Luke 5 looks very promising as his life finds a whole new direction and purpose. However, fast-forward to Luke 22, and the picture we get of Peter is a lot less favourable. His following of Jesus turns into its opposite: a disowning of Jesus. The Gospel doesn't pull its punches in describing him.

Jesus has given the disciples warning after warning about what is to happen, but they don't listen, or misunderstand. In the face of the cross, the disciples are filled with a silly status obsession and competitiveness (v. 24), and Peter himself boasts of how he's willing to die with Jesus (v. 33). His heart is soon exposed as he denies Jesus three times – initially, in front of a powerless slave girl. The tragic finale comes as Jesus himself looks at Peter in the moment of denial (v. 61), and he is left with bitter failure, guilt and tears.

At this point, we might expect the lesson of it all to be that we shouldn't be like Peter – and that is an important and true application of the story. We are indeed challenged here to live out a faithful discipleship in the face of testing circumstances (cf. 9:26). Yet, while we might think that it would be great not to resemble Peter, the fact is that he isn't the worst of believers, but the best. Peter actually tells us more about the tendencies of our hearts than we might like to think. While, then, the story can drive us to renewed vigilance and determined faithfulness, it should, on a deeper level, humble us. Our following is always imperfect, and sometimes the best of us can end up falling into the worst things.

All through this chapter, the betrayal of Judas, and the unfaithfulness of Peter, go hand in hand. The actions of the two characters are interweaved and compared. They have both shared in the ministry of Jesus through preaching and performing miracles. And here, at the end, we see that both are proud (22:24), both repudiate Jesus (vv. 4, 57) and both are being influenced by Satan (vv. 3, 31). That should sober us in many ways. While we might naturally want to draw a very tight distinction between Judas and these other apostles, thinking that Judas' betrayal was about some distinctively awful character defect, the fact is that these men were not fundamentally different. The gospel narrative emphasises their similarities more than we might want to consider.

The real difference between Judas and Peter isn't found in their character as such, but in sovereign grace. In the mystery of God's election, Peter experiences the grace of God preserving him, while Judas is handed over to his sin. We see both salvation and reprobation at work here. Judas' betrayal isn't simply the expression of his own sin, but also the fulfilment of the divine plan (Luke 22:22; Matt. 27:9–10; John 13:18). Peter's preservation, on the other hand, is as much due to divine grace as Judas' betrayal is due to divine rejection. Jesus makes the reality of sovereign grace clear in his response to Peter's arrogant declaration of faithfulness in Luke 22:33. Peter's denial is known and predicted. His hope, in the face of Satan's onslaught, won't be in his faithfulness, but in Jesus' faithful intercession for him. Peter won't uphold his own faith, but Jesus will do it for him. Jesus' words declare the certainty of preservation despite Peter's own unbelief and disobedience.

Our confidence in the robustness of our following is humbled here. There is much potential failure in us, but the grace of God and the intercession of Jesus are the foundations of our hope. Satan will sift us, too, and we shouldn't put much stock in our own zeal and faith to carry us through those seasons. We, too, must beware bold declarations of what we believe ourselves to be. Rather, our confidence is in Jesus' faithful preservation of us, instead of our faithful following of him. Sovereign grace undergirds all true discipleship.

Fishermen or fishers of men?

> Afterwards Jesus appeared again to his disciples, by the Sea of Galilee. It happened this way: Simon Peter, Thomas (also known as Didymus), Nathanael from Cana in Galilee, the sons of Zebedee, and two other disciples were together. 'I'm going out to fish,' Simon Peter told them, and they said, 'We'll go with you.' So they went out and got into the boat, but that night they caught nothing.

Early in the morning, Jesus stood on the shore, but the disciples did not realise that it was Jesus.

He called out to them, 'Friends, haven't you any fish?'

'No,' they answered.

He said, 'Throw your net on the right side of the boat and you will find some.' When they did, they were unable to haul the net in because of the large number of fish.

Then the disciple whom Jesus loved said to Peter, 'It is the Lord!' As soon as Simon Peter heard him say, 'It is the Lord,' he wrapped his outer garment round him (for he had taken it off) and jumped into the water. The other disciples followed in the boat, towing the net full of fish, for they were not far from shore, about a hundred metres. When they landed, they saw a fire of burning coals there with fish on it, and some bread.

Jesus said to them, 'Bring some of the fish you have just caught.' So Simon Peter climbed back into the boat and dragged the net ashore. It was full of large fish, 153, but even with so many the net was not torn. Jesus said to them, 'Come and have breakfast.' None of the disciples dared ask him, 'Who are you?' They knew it was the Lord. Jesus came, took the bread and gave it to them, and did the same with the fish. This was now the third time Jesus appeared to his disciples after he was raised from the dead.

When they had finished eating, Jesus said to Simon Peter, 'Simon son of John, do you love me more than these?'

'Yes, Lord,' he said, 'you know that I love you.'

Jesus said, 'Feed my lambs.'

Again Jesus said, 'Simon son of John, do you love me?'

He answered, 'Yes, Lord, you know that I love you.'

Jesus said, 'Take care of my sheep.'

The third time he said to him, 'Simon son of John, do you love me?'

Peter was hurt because Jesus asked him the third time, 'Do you love me?' He said, 'Lord, you know all things; you know that I love you.'

Jesus said, 'Feed my sheep. Very truly I tell you, when you were younger you dressed yourself and went where you wanted; but when you are old you will stretch out your hands, and someone else will dress you and lead you where you do not want to go.' Jesus said this to indicate the kind of death by which Peter would glorify God. Then he said to him, 'Follow me!'

Peter turned and saw that the disciple whom Jesus loved was following them. (This was

> the one who had leaned back against Jesus at the supper and had said, 'Lord, who is going to betray you?') When Peter saw him, he asked, 'Lord, what about him?'
>
> Jesus answered, 'If I want him to remain alive until I return, what is that to you? You must follow me.' Because of this, the rumour spread among the believers that this disciple would not die. But Jesus did not say that he would not die; he only said, 'If I want him to remain alive until I return, what is that to you?' (John 21:1–23).

John 21 is the fulfilment of Jesus' promise in Luke 22:31–32. Here we see, through the grace of Jesus, that Peter's failure in disowning him is not an ultimate failure. The context is important and obvious. The disciples' confusion, despair and disappointment in the face of the cross is gone as they have met the risen Jesus. Their hearts have, accordingly, been transformed from doubt and fear to joy. The Lord has breathed the Spirit upon them, commissioned them and sent them out in great authority (John 20:21–22).

There is, though, still more for the disciples, particularly Peter, to learn. The story now moves from the inner room in John 20 to the Sea of Galilee in John 21. The disciples are fishing (again). It is unclear to what extent this is to be seen negatively. On the one hand, this could be read as them drifting back to their old lives and sidelining the ministry that the risen Jesus had recently given them. Yet, on the other hand, there isn't any rebuke here from Jesus for their fishing. The story, on balance, seems to be silent on this issue. Whatever their motives or intentions, Peter again finds himself on a rather unsuccessful fishing expedition. This is about more than old skills having become rusty in the intervening years! Here we have another divine intervention.

In verse 4, we read that the risen Jesus is there – though incognito. The disciples don't know it is him, creating the dramatic tension of the story. But Jesus calls out, rather ironically, 'Friends, haven't you any fish?' (v. 5). (It's hard to read this and think that Jesus has no sense of humour.) The question is, in a sense, superfluous as the Lord knows that they haven't caught anything – and he knows why. The disciples answer in the negative, maybe a tad defensively! Jesus then makes what, on the surface of things, seems like a rather ridiculous suggestion: to throw their nets over the right side.

Yet, despite its apparent stupidity, the disciples remarkably do what he asks. Do they have some inkling about him? Or maybe they just want to humble the smart alec on the shore? Whatever the reason, the result is another fishing miracle. The nets become spectacularly full; in fact, so full that the disciples can't haul in all the fish. Of course, they could be forgiven here for thinking they were experiencing déjà vu because they were! Peter's initial encounter with Jesus is repeating itself. It becomes clear that these two fishing miracles function as bookends to the story of

Peter. John 21 should, accordingly, be viewed in light of Luke 5:1–11.[2]

Peter's betrayal and reinstatement now becomes the focus of the story. The repeated miracle is necessary because of what had happened at Jesus' arrest and trial. Peter had reneged on his personal commitment to his Lord, and so he needs to be recommissioned. Jesus is, once again, calling him from being a fisherman to becoming a fisher of men. Though Peter had seen the empty tomb and been with the risen Jesus, there is still more for him to know and learn. Notice that, in John 21, Peter had been fishing in the dark (v. 3), but with Jesus a new day comes (v. 12). Light is now dawning in Peter's darkness.

In reaction to the miracle, the disciples' eyes are opened ('It is the Lord!' v. 7). They see who this man on the shore is, and Peter, who had previously retreated from Jesus, now runs to him. Though tremendous, the catch of fish is insignificant. The sign fades into the background before the One to whom it is pointing. Peter leaves his boat and nets once again for Jesus. He is recovering his call to follow the Lord.

Stepping onto land, the disciples receive a gracious invitation from the risen Lord: 'Come and have breakfast' (v. 12). Here we see the first ever men's breakfast as the disciples enjoy Jesus' remarkable hospitality. There are echoes of feeding miracles as well as fishing miracles. We're told that there were 153 fish in the net (v. 11), which amounts to nineteen fish per person! The sheer amount of food points to the Lord's remarkable abundance for his people. This was truly an 'all-you-can-eat' buffet with a large amount of leftovers. Jesus' gracious provision for them again is a reminder that he can give us more than we ever ask for or imagine (Eph. 3:20–21). Fishers of men will never lack ample supply for their own needs.

Do you love me?

In John 21:15–23, we come to Jesus' famous questions to Peter. Here the Lord's grace is wonderfully poured out over Peter's life as he is reinstated and recommissioned as a spiritual leader. Jesus fulfils the prediction he made in Luke 22:31–32. Three times the question 'do you love me?' is asked, paralleling Peter's three denials. His failure and sin have been plunged into the cross. What might have seemed impossible a short time earlier is now made possible: he will be restored to leadership. What an incredible conclusion to this story and what a hope for failed leaders! Nothing is impossible with the Lord. In our worst moments, and in our failures, the Lord Jesus can still come to us with restoring grace.

However, though this grace is fantastic, it isn't easygoing; there is discipline and challenge as well. Here the one who had been renamed Cephas/Peter ('the rock') is addressed by his original name, 'Simon son of Jonah' (v. 15). He clearly hasn't been the rock he had been called to be. Further, while the thrice-asked question is a reinstatement, it is also a reminder of his denial. The questions are, in other words, piercing. They wound as well as comfort: 'Peter was hurt because Jesus asked him the third time, "Do you love me?"' (v. 17). There is tremendous grace, but it isn't cheap. Thus, we see that the reinstatement of leaders after significant failure, even directly by the Lord Jesus, is not a simple process. On the one hand, significant failure doesn't have to become ultimate failure, and yet, on the other hand, the covering of that failure is difficult. There is hope for us all, even while we are sobered by the realities of sin and grace.

The sobering realities of Peter's reinstatement become clear in verses 18–19 as Jesus calls him to do the very thing that he had backed off from before: to die in service of his Lord. It's a very moving and holy scene. Peter has just been asked three times, 'do you love me?' In John 15:13, Jesus had defined love as laying down our lives for our friends. That is exactly what Jesus has done, but it is exactly what Peter has not done. Peter will be called to show a love for Jesus by living out that pattern of self-sacrifice and death.

Alongside the thrice-asked question about love, Peter is commanded three times to do the work of a shepherd and care for the sheep. The image has a sobering background because, in John 10:11, Jesus has already defined what shepherding the flock really means: it too means laying down one's life. Feeding the sheep and spiritual friendship aren't then, as we might imagine, just about preparing a good sermon, but are about dying for those who are precious to the Lord. At the heart of all ministry – of any kind – is the sacrifice of oneself for others. Peter is told that the hands that feed the lambs will be stretched out for Jesus in crucifixion. Just as Jesus had glorified the Father in his death (17:4), Peter will glorify God in his crucifixion (21:19). Reinstatement to leadership isn't about regaining position, power and privilege, but about being reinstated to follow our Lord in the way of the cross.

Following Jesus now sounds quite different to how it might have sounded in Luke 5:11 and John 1:43! It is actually all about following him all the way to the cross. While we might naturally feel that it would be amazing to meet the risen Jesus, when he asks us to do things like this, we might suddenly not feel so keen to meet him any more! This interaction with Peter makes it clear that there really isn't anything that the Lord Jesus can't ask us to do. Surely, Peter didn't sing, 'I love Jesus' quite so glibly after that, and neither should we.

His will, your story

As Peter ponders his future, his mind immediately goes to the other disciples, in particular the 'disciple whom Jesus loved' (21:20). Peter asks, 'Lord, what about him?' (v. 21). Jesus has outlined Peter's destiny, and the question that naturally arises is how much this will be a pattern for all disciples. Jesus' reply is both mysterious and corrective: 'Jesus answered, "If I want him to remain alive until I return, what is that to you? You must follow me"' (v. 22).

C. S. Lewis alludes to this scene in *The Horse and His Boy*, one his Narnia books. The heroes, a girl called Aravis and a boy called Shasta, are racing by horse to Narnia to save it from the nasty Calormenes. On the way, they are chased by a mysterious lion, who hounds them at every point. When they are almost there, the lion catches them and, rising up, tears at Aravis's shoulder with great strength. Aravis screams with her back now covered in blood. Later in the story, they meet Aslan the lion, the guardian of Narnia. Aslan tells Shasta that he was the one who badly hurt Aravis. Shasta's natural shock leads him to ask why on earth Aslan would do such a thing? Wasn't he meant to be on their side?! Aslan's reply is very instructive for our passage: 'Child, I am telling you your story, not hers. I tell no one any story but his own.'[3]

Jesus is Lord, and he is in charge. He doesn't tell us what someone else will do, and that's not our concern. They are, after all, his servants and not ours. What matters is whether or not we will follow Jesus in what he has laid out for us. Maybe the Lord will give others a comfortable and easy life, and send us on a difficult path. Or maybe he won't. It is simply up to him. Given this, we can be tempted to make rules for others according to what the Lord has called us to do. We can want others to give up what we have given up, and call others to suffer as we have suffered. Yet, we must resist this and simply concern ourselves with the story to which the Lord has called us. Whatever we must face, Jesus says, 'You must follow me' (v. 22). Let's take up our crosses and do that.

– 2 –

Loving Jesus

To be a disciple of Jesus is to love Jesus. He is at the centre of all their affection and joy. On a very basic level, every leader, before they lead anything, is such a disciple. Spiritual leadership isn't an escape from basic discipleship, but, on the contrary, an intensification of it. At the heart of all true spiritual leadership, then, is a love for Jesus.

In reading this, you're probably not falling off your chair in amazement. Nor are you thinking, 'Why has no one ever told me this before? What? Love Jesus?! I'll go and do that straight away!' You hopefully know very well that you are called to love Jesus. This is obvious and elementary teaching, and the most basic of discipleship lessons. Yet, as leaders, we also know that right in the middle of speaking about Jesus to others, and making him known to the world, our love for him can fade and disappear. Though we're planting churches in all kinds of new unreached places and seeing tremendous success, and though we're expounding

God's word to crowds, we can also find that our joy in him becomes strangely dimmed.

There can be many reasons for this joylessness, but the strange irony is that ministry for Jesus can itself be the big drain on our love for him. Over time, for example, we can become cynical and rather jaded. This can be a particular danger for older leaders. When we're younger, the danger we face is pride and presumption, but, over the years, we can move more towards discouragement and disappointment. Experience can make us feel our own failures, and the failures of those around us. We were once full of expectation, but it can seem that many don't respond to the gospel and that we don't see the conversions we wanted. Trusted brothers and sisters fall away from the faith, or leaders who we admired fall into scandal. As a result, our love for Jesus can take a beating from the brutal realities of a fallen world, and we can find ourselves unbalanced in faith and life. We slowly wind down and the fire grows cold as we start to give up. Ministry can, sadly, undo us.

Yet, this isn't a new temptation. A few hundred years ago, the wise and godly pastor John Newton penned some sobering words:

> It is, indeed, no small thing to stand between God and the people, to divide the word of truth aright, to give every one their portion, to withstand the counter tides of opposition and popularity, and to press those truths upon others, the power of which, I, at times, feel so little of in my own

> soul. A cold, corrupt heart is uncomfortable company in the pulpit.[1]

In another letter, he writes this:

> When our dear Lord questioned Peter, after his fall and recovery, he did not say, 'Are you wise, learned, and eloquent?' No! He did not say, 'Are you clear and sound, and orthodox?' But this only, 'Do you love me?'[2]

So, despite our clarity, soundness and orthodoxy, we would be wise to recognise that, in the middle of ministry for Jesus, we can find ourselves without much actual love for him. This will leave us empty and hollow, living out a duty without devotion, and an allegiance without affection. Such ministry becomes a soul-destroying, loveless marriage. Hypocrisy will follow fast as the gap between our outward profession and our inward life becomes greater and greater.

For some, a lack of love for Jesus will simply lead us into an infatuation with ourselves:

> But mark this: there will be terrible times in the last days. People will be *lovers of themselves, lovers of money,* boastful, proud, abusive, disobedient to their parents, ungrateful, unholy, *without love,* unforgiving, slanderous, without self-control, brutal, *not lovers of the good,*

> treacherous, rash, conceited, *lovers of pleasure rather than lovers of God* (2 Tim. 3:1–4, my emphasis).

Such leaders cease to be true pastors and preachers of God's word, but become actors performing for the crowd and pleasing themselves. Their life becomes a 'resounding gong or a clanging cymbal' (1 Cor. 13:1) as they fail to love Jesus or other people.

Wonderfully loved

Looking at our own hearts can quickly leave us feeling fairly depressed. However, despite all our coldness and apathy, it is wonderful to know that our starting point with Jesus isn't our love for him, but his love for us. The gospel is good news about his compassion, not our devotion. So, while we can easily find ourselves discouraged by our lack of affection for him, we can, at the same time, be very encouraged by his lavish, enduring commitment to us. He has united us to himself (Eph. 2:6), poured out his love upon us by the Spirit (Rom. 5:5) and now holds us in an unbreakable covenant (Heb. 10:15–16). Nothing can separate us from his love (Rom. 8:38–39).

Do you feel that the Lord's affection towards you is more like a cool, begrudging acceptance? Does your Christian life seem like one long attempt to win the approval of a distant headmaster? Do you live in the joyless gloom of an imagined omnipotent, omnipresent frown? Well, fantastically, the word of God speaks authoritatively over us and proclaims Jesus' gut-wrenching love for us.[3] Luke's Gospel tells us what this gut-wrenching love looks like:

- It is the Saviour's compassion for a widow at the funeral of her only child (Luke 7:13).
- It is the Samaritan serving a beaten-up Jew on the side of the road (Luke 10:33).
- It is the Father's reaction to his prodigal son (Luke 15:20).

It's not just the people we lead who need to know that the Lord loves them; we need to know it too! We leaders need a realisation that we are loved like this, even if we're an ex-SAS superman who eats pastoral problems for breakfast! Our enthusiasm, joy, toughness and perseverance depend upon knowing this. But, most important of all, our great privilege as disciples and leaders is we get to bask in his love. So, why would we ever neglect it? As Spurgeon says:

> It is the distinguishing mark of God's people that they know the love of Christ. Without exception all those who have passed from death unto life, whatever they may not know, have learned this. Without exception, all those who are not saved, whatever they may know besides, know nothing of this. An ungodly man may know something about Christ's love; he may believe in the fact of it; he may perceive some-

> thing of the theory of it. He may even be able to follow believers in certain expressions of its enjoyments. But to know the love itself, to taste its sweets, to realise personally, experimentally, and vitally, the love of Christ as shed abroad in our hearts by the Holy Ghost, is the privilege of the child of God, and of the child of God alone.[4]

At the feet of Jesus

Leaders are called to live in a relationship of love with Jesus. We get a vivid depiction of this relationship in three different encounters with Jesus in Luke's Gospel. The striking thing in each is that the person concerned is left at the feet of Jesus – being loved by him and loving him. Luke's Gospel won't leave us standing up, feeling tall and strong. Only the proud stand in the presence of Jesus, while the humble, broken sinner finds themselves down in the dust. And it is precisely this person who finds the grace of God working so powerfully in their lives. We learn that we have to bend the knee and get low to look at Jesus. It's no accident that the Greek word for worship, *proskuneō*, means 'bending the knee'. The big lesson for us as we look at these encounters is that real spiritual leadership never gets beyond this basic posture. Leadership is lived out on its knees before Jesus.

Extravagant love

> When one of the Pharisees invited Jesus to have dinner with him, he went to the Pharisee's

house and reclined at the table. A woman in that town who lived a sinful life learned that Jesus was eating at the Pharisee's house, so she came there with an alabaster jar of perfume. As she stood behind him at his feet weeping, she began to wet his feet with her tears. Then she wiped them with her hair, kissed them and poured perfume on them.

When the Pharisee who had invited him saw this, he said to himself, 'If this man were a prophet, he would know who is touching him and what kind of woman she is – that she is a sinner.'

Jesus answered him, 'Simon, I have something to tell you.'

'Tell me, teacher,' he said.

'Two people owed money to a certain money-lender. One owed him five hundred denarii, and the other fifty. Neither of them had the money to pay him back, so he forgave the debts of both. Now which of them will love him more?'

Simon replied, 'I suppose the one who had the bigger debt forgiven.'

'You have judged correctly,' Jesus said.

Then he turned towards the woman and said to Simon, 'Do you see this woman? I came into your house. You did not give me any water for my feet, but she wet my feet with her tears and wiped them with her hair. You did not give me a kiss, but this woman, from the time I entered, has not stopped

> kissing my feet. You did not put oil on my head, but she has poured perfume on my feet. Therefore, I tell you, her many sins have been forgiven – as her great love has shown. But whoever has been forgiven little loves little.'
>
> Then Jesus said to her, 'Your sins are forgiven.'
>
> The other guests began to say among themselves, 'Who is this who even forgives sins?'
>
> Jesus said to the woman, 'Your faith has saved you; go in peace' (Luke 7:36–50).

The first story of a 'bended knee' for us to consider is this famous account of the sinful woman at the feet of Jesus. There are few stories that move us and stir us like it. Yet, it is hugely challenging, as it presents an absolutely devastating contrast between the cool, detached engagement of a well-taught old-covenant teacher, and the extravagant, risky devotion of what many would have seen as a silly, hysterical, promiscuous woman.

As a Pharisee, Simon had a reputation and spiritual gravitas. He knew his Scriptures intimately and was zealous for God's laws. His life was moral, distinctive and separate from the corruption around him. It seems that Simon was also spiritually interested, and engaged with Jesus and his teaching. He apparently wanted to know more about this new rabbi who had appeared on the scene (much like Nicodemus in John 3). However, we should also note that his engagement with Jesus was distanced, cool and detached. He was happy to listen and interact with Jesus, but he wasn't devoted to him, as Jesus himself points out. Jesus describes the heart of the Pharisees at other points in Luke's Gospel, and this helps us understand what is driving Simon in this story:

> Woe to you Pharisees, because you love the most important seats in the synagogues and respectful greetings in the market-places (Luke 11:43).

> Beware of the teachers of the law. They like to walk around in flowing robes and love to be greeted with respect in the market-places and have the most important seats in the synagogues and the places of honour at banquets (Luke 20:46).

Simon was a man who would have loved flowing robes, respect, contact with the right leaders and being known by the right people. Simon was the kind of man who would have enjoyed having a place of significance and honour at old-covenant ministerial conferences. He loved many things – but he just didn't love Jesus.

The woman is a huge contrast to Simon. She's not a minister, but a woman with utterly negative spiritual credentials. We don't know if she was a prostitute, but she seemed to have an awful reputation. In an honour-and-shame culture, she would have been an 'untouchable'. Yet, it is this woman who gives an amazing example of extravagant love for Jesus. Her approach was shameless, public and passionate.

To update this for a twenty-first-century context, let's imagine that a violent skinhead with swastika tattoos comes into our church. He's had a reputation for attacking locals, but now declares his faith in Jesus and raises his arms to sing loudly about him. Understandably, many might be wary or concerned about such a man coming into their gathering – and how that might impact the church's relationship with the local community. Would we trust this man – particularly if we knew people who he had put into hospital?

The scene in Luke 7 is certainly full of 'over-the-top' and scandalous emotional drama. The woman may have seemed fanatical, or a tad unhinged. She literally lets down her hair (maybe a cultural sign of promiscuity) and lavishes expensive perfume (maybe part of her trade if she was a sex worker) on Jesus. She wipes his feet and blubbers all over him (the original Greek word here could be used for rain showers). Whatever people's perception, she doesn't really seem to give much notice. In fact, her lack of self-consciousness or fear of others' opinion is really quite remarkable. The fact is that she's too busy loving Jesus to think about it. Further, notice how Jesus does absolutely nothing to stop her. He's not in the least awkward, nor does he tell her off. There are no lectures or sermons about purity, decorum and the 'dangers of emotionalism'. Jesus seems to welcome her approach.

This whole scene is too much for Simon, though. Here we have an upstanding, zealous Bible teacher. He's a man concerned for obedience and purity – and this is *his* house. The woman's behaviour simply can*not* go on! The whole tone of this is reminiscent of an episode of *The Simpsons* where Homer Simpson's fundamentalist Christian neighbours had been away on a trip. Homer asks them where they have been, and they reply, 'We went away to Christian camp. We were learning to be more judgmental.' Simon would have fitted right in. Surely, he thinks, if Jesus were a *true* prophet, he would know who this was and he'd tell her off. Surely, Jesus would at least get rid of her?! In Simon's mind, this is a test for Jesus, but, in reality, this woman is a test for Simon's own heart. It is Simon, and not the woman, who is going to get the sermon here in verses 44–47.

The teacher is thus exposed by Jesus. His hospitality has been superficial – welcoming Jesus into his house, but not into his life. He knows the Law, but he hasn't lavished anything on Jesus. Simon is happy to have a debate, but isn't interested in devoting himself to Jesus. He has lukewarm religion – in contrast to the woman's passionate, public love.

It's striking that the model for all of us here isn't the educated, smart, well-taught Bible teacher, but the seemingly hysterical woman of dubious character. This is not who we expect to be held up as a model disciple! Her devotion, though, is deeply convicting for our hearts. We should stop for a moment and ask ourselves whether anyone could ever accuse us of being like this woman? Might anyone ever criticise us for being over the top in our love for Jesus? Could we ever be thought of as being just a bit too much when it comes to our devotion? We are being alerted to the ever-present danger of being dutiful but lukewarm. The risk is that our reserved, restrained emotions and reasonableness are more like an imitation of Simon. People may appreciate our calmness, but that could just be a cloak for a cold heart. We may do and say the right things, and preach with piercing clarity, yet we may also do it all with hearts that are unengaged and uninspired. There might be no obvious, terrible sins in our lives, but is there 'crazy' passion? Some of us need to go and find our alabaster jars, break them and let down our hair!

As we come to the end of the story, it's striking to read that the root of this woman's extravagance is in a profound experience of forgiveness. That's the point of the little parable tucked away in verses 40–43. The woman's brokenness before the all-forgiving Saviour has been transformative for her. The eradication of her spiritual debt has proved to be rocket fuel for her devotion. Notice that this story isn't sentimental about the woman. She is treated as a real sinner, with real spiritual debts. But we learn here the simple principle that the size of the debt that's been relieved stands in direct proportion to the love that is generated. If I give you £5 to cover a debt, you'll offer me a quick thanks and then move on. If I give you £500, then you might write me a card and offer a serious 'thank you'. If I give you £5000, then you'll be my friend for life. If I give you £500,000, then you will be tempted to fall down and worship me! The size of the debt that's been relieved always has a huge impact on the gratitude produced. The woman knows that she has been relieved of an overwhelming debt and that changes everything.

Simon, on the other hand, experiences no such relief, and thus no great love. His self-righteousness and self-confidence is the rocket fuel for his own cool detachment. His Bible teaching and religious zeal have, ironically, left him impervious to gospel truth. Rather than being humbled and broken by his sin, his religion has seared his conscience so that he can't really see his own sin. He stands before the Judge of all, and judges him for perceived permissiveness. He talks with the Teacher, but cannot heed the lesson.

We mustn't treat Jesus as if he has just lent us a fiver! At the heart of all healthy spiritual leadership is a continual return to the grace of the Saviour. We live not by our works, but by his mercy. Be refreshed with that, and love will be rekindled in your heart.

Sane love

> They sailed to the region of the Gerasenes, which is across the lake from Galilee. When Jesus stepped ashore, he was met by a demon-possessed man from the town. For a long time this man had not worn clothes or lived in a house, but had lived in the tombs. When he saw

Jesus, he cried out and fell at his feet, shouting at the top of his voice, 'What do you want with me, Jesus, Son of the Most High God? I beg you, don't torture me!' For Jesus had commanded the impure spirit to come out of the man. Many times it had seized him, and though he was chained hand and foot and kept under guard, he had broken his chains and had been driven by the demon into solitary places.

Jesus asked him, 'What is your name?'

'Legion,' he replied, because many demons had gone into him. And they begged Jesus repeatedly not to order them to go into the Abyss.

A large herd of pigs was feeding there on the hillside. The demons begged Jesus to let them go into the pigs, and he gave them permission. When the demons came out of the man, they went into the pigs, and the herd rushed down the steep bank into the lake and was drowned.

When those tending the pigs saw what had happened, they ran off and reported this in the town and countryside, and the people went out to see what had happened. When they came to Jesus, they found the man from whom the demons had gone out, sitting at Jesus' feet, dressed and in his right mind; and they were afraid. Those who had seen it told the people how the demon-possessed man had been

> cured. Then all the people of the region of the Gerasenes asked Jesus to leave them, because they were overcome with fear. So he got into the boat and left.
>
> The man from whom the demons had gone out begged to go with him, but Jesus sent him away, saying, 'Return home and tell how much God has done for you.' So the man went away and told all over the town how much Jesus had done for him (Luke 8:26–39).

Just a few verses on from the woman anointing Jesus in Luke 7, we have the equally moving story of the demoniac, Legion. In many ways, this is a very striking contrast; while the woman's encounter with Jesus makes her extravagant, emotional and radical in her devotion, Legion's encounter with Jesus does precisely the opposite. The woman's encounter, motivated by the grace of Jesus, makes her 'crazy' in her love, whereas Legion's encounter with Jesus makes him calm. The woman breaks her alabaster jar, lets down her hair and weeps for joy, but Legion is simply clothed. There is, again, emotional drama here, but this second encounter is characterised by sanity rather than wildness. This is a beautiful story about a broken man being restored as he ends up at the feet of Jesus in true submission and peace.

Legion starts off isolated, alone and profoundly oppressed in verse 27 and 29. He is a kind of distorted Samson figure, overwhelmed with dangerous strength from evil spirits. We have here a horrible picture of spiritual slavery and self-destruction. If you've ever worked with drug users or serious alcoholics, you might have had a taste of this brokenness. It is spiritual slavery worked out to an extreme.[5] It is a taste of hell on earth. Here we meet a lost man, filled with unclean spirits, who comes from an unclean community (Gerasenes was a Gentile region). He lives with unclean animals (pigs) in an unclean area (a graveyard). Everything is defiled and offensive to the holy, pure presence of God; this is a spiritually foul place. According to typical Jewish piety, keeping yourself clear of it would be a very good idea.

Yet, this is precisely where the Lord chooses to come – crossing sea and land to get to the region. We know that the Son of God doesn't do anything by accident or chance, so he must intentionally come for *just* this Gentile demoniac. Soon after, he will cross back to the other side and continue with his ministry in Israel. But now Jesus makes a deliberate detour, through a storm (Luke 8:22–25), to get to this man. He heads straight into this defiled, offensive, foul scene to rescue this broken, enslaved demoniac. We will see that Jesus, rather than being overwhelmed and contaminated by the uncleanness, is the Pure One who overwhelms the spiritually dirty with his own cleanness.

We have to have some sympathy for the poor disciples, though, as they land here. They've just been frightened witless by the storm, had a near-death experience and been told off by Jesus. They land, drenched, recovering from their collective panic attack and looking forward to firm ground to stand on. And, immediately, a naked, demonised man, with superpower strength, comes running towards them. What do they do? Go back onto the lake where they might get drowned in another storm, or face down the wild eyed he-man?! They are about to get a firm object lesson in the incredible, supreme power of the Lord Jesus.

This is the most detailed exorcism account in the whole of Scripture. We might expect gory details, but it's rather disappointing for the director of horror films. This doesn't become some dualistic duel to the death, but is just instant deliverance through the omnipotence of Jesus. There's no paraphernalia – no holy water, nor holding up of a battered Bible. There's no hocus pocus, spinning heads or levitating bodies. On the contrary, the word of Jesus simply delivers this poor, oppressed and broken man from an army of devils in a second.

The result is remarkable. Verse 35 paints a beautiful scene where nakedness, chaos and demons have been replaced by clothes, sanity and the presence of Jesus. The man who lived among the tombs is now sent back to his community to live among his family. Here we have a broken, degraded life that has been plunged into the power and grace of Jesus, and the man comes up transformed. He finds the feet of Jesus to be a place of rest, recuperation and refreshment. Instead of being driven by demons, he is now filled with sane love for Jesus.

As we read this story, we understandably feel that our lives are (thankfully!) quite far from Legion's experience. After all, we're quite capable of dressing ourselves and sleeping in a bed (and not the local graveyard). We also, on our good days, reckon ourselves to be reasonably sane! Yet, there are times, surely, when we aren't in our right minds? We know that the pressure and struggle in ministry can undo us as we live in a spiritual war, and the enemy is active. He tempts us and sends his messengers into our ministries. Accordingly, there are seasons, for a whole range of reasons, when we become stressed, angry and depressed – maybe more Legion-like than we would care to admit? We can start to lose perspective and our tempers. We might start to lash out at people, bang tables in anger and drink too much. We don't have superhuman strength, yet we start to bully others.

This story reminds us, though, that there is rest for us at the feet of Jesus. We need to linger and take time there. We need to come to him, being loved by him and loving him. He is supremely powerful as he acts for us and his word will set us free. The Lord Jesus will settle us, dress us and give us our sanity back. He will send us back out, in a life of sane love and devotion, with restored minds. Here we have an almighty resource to uphold us, and neglect of it will be disastrous. There are many reasons for burnout, but disregarding this fellowship with Jesus has got to be top of the list. He calls us out of spiritual lunacy and back to him.

Listening devotion

> As Jesus and his disciples were on their way, he came to a village where a woman named Martha opened her home to him. She had a sister called Mary, who sat at the Lord's feet listening to what he said. But Martha was distracted by all the preparations that had to be made. She came to him and asked, 'Lord, don't you care that my sister has left me to do the work by myself? Tell her to help me!'
>
> 'Martha, Martha,' the Lord answered, 'you are worried and upset about many things, but few things are needed – or indeed only one. Mary has chosen what is better, and it will not be taken away from her' (Luke 10:38–42).

Martha seems to do everything right in this story, doesn't she? She's hospitable, servant-hearted and hard-working. She's a completer-finisher, a do-er and an activist. In fact, she's just the kind of person we would love to have on our team! She's the kind of person who would start up new ministries, work efficiently and organise everyone. Yet, rather shockingly, Jesus tells us that she doesn't have the one thing that is needed: to sit at the feet of Jesus and listen.

In Luke 10:27, Jesus has already answered a question from an expert in the Law, stating that the great commandments were about loving God and loving our neighbour.

The expert then wanted an answer as to what it meant to live out the second commandment: to love your neighbour. Accordingly, Jesus told him the famous parable of the Good Samaritan. However, in Luke 10:38–42, we also get an answer as to what it means to obey the first commandment: we love God by sitting at the feet of Jesus to listen.

Notice that Martha isn't doing bad things in this story – she hasn't committed immorality, nor has she stolen from Jesus' kitty! Her problem, rather, is that she is failing to pay attention to Jesus. She's on her feet, running around, achieving things, but she's not where she needs to be. Jesus corrects her, telling her that she's worried and upset about many things because she's not doing the one thing that is needed: loving Jesus by listening to him.

Taking time to listen to Jesus is actually a much bigger problem than we think. Ministry attracts Marthas. Activists easily end up being drawn into leadership in churches and other groups. There is also a danger that as we get more responsibility and influence as spiritual leaders, we talk more. We get too used to the sound of our own voice. We become talkers and stop being listeners. This is bad enough when it comes to how we relate to other people, but it becomes a real problem when it shapes our relationship with Jesus. So, we should beware that, while we might do and say great things, we may also be very distracted from the One who really matters. Is it not a frightening thought that we can become a significant leader, with influence and renown, teaching others God's word, and yet fail to mediate on the word ourselves? We might end up doing and talking all the time, but not listening to him.

Of course, if we stop for a moment and sit down at Jesus' feet, the preparations probably won't get done. The food might be dicey and the plates will pile up. But, encouragingly, the real work will get done. Let's be a Mary. Let's go to Jesus' word so that we live out the one thing that really matters.

Down in the dirt

Every leader is called to live a life at the feet of Jesus, being loved by him and loving him. We will find that getting down in the dirt isn't so bad when he's there. In fact, this is just where we belong. Jesus wants leaders who are not on their feet, but at his feet. If we want to know him, we have to bow the knee. And as we do that, we will receive his great love for us. If we still have qualms about doing this, we should remember that Jesus got down in the dirt for us long before we ever got low before him.

We've thought about the extravagant love of the sinful woman, but, at the end of the day, the real extravagance in that story isn't hers, but Jesus'. He is the extravagant One who laid himself down for us. He didn't just let down his hair, but he took off his kingly glory and stepped onto the cross. The cost of his love was more than an alabaster jar; it was his very life that was broken for our salvation.

We wonder at Jesus' concern for one, lost, demonised man, Legion, and we are in awe of his power to set him free. Yet, remarkably, Jesus showed the extent of his love and power by eventually becoming like Legion at another foul, unclean place: Golgotha. There he too was driven out of the city, stripped naked, cut and bound – for us. Jesus crossed much more than just a lake for us – he traversed the infinite distance from heaven to earth. He took our foul, unclean lives upon himself so that we might sit at his feet, dressed in him and in our right minds.

The point is that Jesus was down in the dirt for us long before we ever get down there ourselves. Love for Jesus is absolutely key and central to all leadership, but even more basic and fundamental is his love for us. We follow and get on our knees for a Saviour who humbled himself for us first.

– 3 –

Depending on Jesus

We all long to be effective, impact the world, leave a legacy and see people spiritually changed. However, though we want spiritual power to have that impact, we must also wrestle with the paradox that spiritual power comes from dependence rather than strength, prowess or gifting. In John 15:4, Jesus effectively says to his disciples that without him they can do nothing. That really should be the slogan for the whole of our ministry. Our call isn't to self-reliance, but to Christ-reliance. Great leaders, biblically speaking, are needy people.

Neediness doesn't seem a very positive trait for us. It's not the most flattering description of someone, and hardly a label we would want attached to ourselves as leaders. The needy people (as we perceive them) in our congregation, student group or Bible study are not the people we're most drawn towards. After all, these are the people who absorb our energy, and make our heart sink when they approach.

We often find ourselves having to 'dig deep' just to love them. Who, therefore, wants to be needy?!

Scripture, however, teaches us that neediness is a very positive trait – and actually a necessity for leadership. Dependence and neediness are at the heart of all true spiritual vitality. We're not the omni-competent high achievers we might like to think. Rather, our Christian lives (including our leadership) are, in essence, one long act of dependence upon Jesus for all his benefits, life and power. If I can lead, envision, pastor, evangelise and plant churches without Jesus, then is what I'm doing really worthwhile? We are tempted to think that the greatest obstacle to our leadership is a lack of resources, circumstances or people, but surely the greatest threat of all is a lack of dependence on Jesus. We must beware in ourselves a growing sense of independence and godless self-confidence. Such self-confidence says, 'I can do it, my gifts are enough and my experience is sufficient.'

This is not just a word for the obviously self-reliant, though. Ironically, a lack of self-confidence can be just as self-oriented and self-regarding. In chronic self-doubt, anxiety and fear, I can also be manifesting a real sense of spiritual independence because I still view myself at the centre of my world. Even if I feel that I'm the failure, I'm focusing on myself as the source of my reliance.

Whatever my particular battles – whether I have too much or too little self-confidence – the call is away from myself to growing dependence upon Jesus.

Made dependent

None of this should surprise us because we've been made dependent. Genesis 2:7 tells us that we're made of dust. Elsewhere, the Bible uses the images of grass, breath and vapour to describe who we are (Isa. 40:6–8; Ps. 62:9; James 4:14). In other words, we're not supermen or superwomen, but weak, frail and easily overcome. Notice that this isn't simply the result of the Fall, but it is how we've been designed! Accordingly, this basic dependence isn't something that we will lose in heaven, as we will never be self-existing or self-sustaining. That's why we can't just take a breath filled with oxygen and then keep going for the rest of our lives. God hasn't just given us a one-off deposit of life for all our days, but upholds us continually. Dependence, therefore, has to be the first virtue of every human being. Rather than being something that we have to be saved from, it's part of God's purpose for us.

We need, then, to be careful that we don't lose a basic sense that, while leaders, we are primarily creatures. We mustn't let power, the praise of others nor success go to our heads. It has often struck me that lots of success early on in ministry is something of a trial. When you find that everything that you touch turns to gold, you can really start to think that *you* are the one who is turning it into gold. It's easy for us to re-enact the Garden of Eden by starting to take on the attributes of God. We forget that we're limited and finite. We're seduced by the serpent's whisper, 'you too can be like God', and start to think that we're invincible and almighty. This lie will lead not only to a character distorted by pride, but to burnout. Limits, which the Lord has placed on me for my good, won't be respected as I seek to be everywhere, do everything and know all things. I will, in that moment, be trying to escape God's design for me.

Desperate dependence

> Now when Jesus returned, a crowd welcomed him, for they were all expecting him. Then a man named Jairus, a synagogue leader, came and fell at Jesus' feet, pleading with him to come to his house because his only daughter, a girl of about twelve, was dying.
>
> As Jesus was on his way, the crowds almost crushed him. And a woman was there who had been subject to bleeding for twelve years, but no one could heal her. She came up behind him and touched the edge of his cloak, and immediately her bleeding stopped.
>
> 'Who touched me?' Jesus asked.
>
> When they all denied it, Peter said, 'Master, the people are crowding and pressing against you.'
>
> But Jesus said, 'Someone touched me; I know that power has gone out from me.'
>
> Then the woman, seeing that she could not go unnoticed, came trembling and fell at

> his feet. In the presence of all the people, she told why she had touched him and how she had been instantly healed. Then he said to her, 'Daughter, your faith has healed you. Go in peace.'
>
> While Jesus was still speaking, someone came from the house of Jairus, the synagogue leader. 'Your daughter is dead,' he said. 'Don't bother the teacher anymore.'
>
> Hearing this, Jesus said to Jairus, 'Don't be afraid; just believe, and she will be healed.'
>
> When he arrived at the house of Jairus, he did not let anyone go in with him except Peter, John and James, and the child's father and mother. Meanwhile, all the people were wailing and mourning for her. 'Stop wailing,' Jesus said. 'She is not dead but asleep.'
>
> They laughed at him, knowing that she was dead. But he took her by the hand and said, 'My child, get up!' Her spirit returned, and at once she stood up. Then Jesus told them to give her something to eat. Her parents were astonished, but he ordered them not to tell anyone what had happened (Luke 8:40–56).

In this passage, we have two intertwined stories, but the clear theme running throughout is one of desperation in the face of sickness and suffering. First of all, we meet

Jairus, an honoured and respected local religious leader. Initially, he is facing his daughter's terrible sickness. He then experiences every parent's worst nightmare – the death of his child. Secondly, we meet the anonymous woman who is 'bleeding' (probably, in modern medical jargon, something like a uterine haemorrhage), and consequently barren. Childlessness, in this historical context, was a kind of ongoing death, bringing shame and isolation in a culture where identity was built on family and kin. This bleeding would also have made her ceremonially unclean, leading to exclusion from the spiritual life of God's people. Lastly, she would have been poor, having spent all her money on quack doctors.[1]

The two people in the story are utterly different from each other, yet they are bound together by a number of things. They both obviously have incredible need. They both also find themselves in a rather curious 'coincidence': the girl is *twelve* years old, and the woman has been suffering for *twelve* years. Above all, they are both bound together by a desperate faith. Jairus humiliates himself at the feet of Jesus, pleading for his daughter's healing. The woman is more indirect, 'sneaking up' on Jesus to get a miracle. Of course, the ancient world had no recourse to modern medical care, and so both would have been at the end of their wits. They were jointly being compelled to trust Jesus in their circumstances.

Yet, the striking thing in this story is how Jesus ends up demanding from them a level of trust that they don't really want to have! We see that Jairus has enough faith to trust Jesus for a healing, but ends up having to trust him to raise the dead. The woman who touches Jesus wants to escape unseen and unnoticed. Jesus, however, catches her red-handed, like a naughty schoolgirl, and she is forced to acknowledge him publicly. Remarkably, though, just as Jesus demands from them a faith that they don't really want to have, he ends up giving them more than they ever imagined! Wonderfully, we see how Jesus' extraordinary power meets their impossible need.

If we want to know Jesus' extraordinary power in our ministries, we need to bottle this kind of neediness. The fragilities, failures, sicknesses and sufferings we experience as leaders aren't impossible obstacles (as much as it feels that they are!), but are the means by which we will learn to be truly dependent. We don't have to be capable and self-reliant, nor do we have to cope well. We just need to be needy. John Newton said, 'When we first enter into the divine life, we propose to grow rich; God's plan is to make us feel poor.'[2] We naturally hate the things that block growth in our ministry and we hate feeling incapable and ignorant. But this is all God's plan to make us feel poor and empty; he is determined that we will know who we really are. Hopefully, it won't take us twelve years of going to quack doctors to learn this. Along the way, though, God may call us to have a desperate faith that we don't really want – in order for us to get a much bigger blessing. Jairus and the unknown woman teach us the discipline of throwing ourselves at Jesus' feet.

Dependence in prayer

> As Jesus approached Jericho, a blind man was sitting by the roadside begging. When he heard the crowd going by, he asked what was happening. They told him, 'Jesus of Nazareth is passing by.'
>
> He called out, 'Jesus, Son of David, have mercy on me!'
>
> Those who led the way rebuked him and told him to be quiet, but he shouted all the more, 'Son of David, have mercy on me!'
>
> Jesus stopped and ordered the man to be brought to him. When he came near, Jesus asked him, 'What do you want me to do for you?'
>
> 'Lord, I want to see,' he replied.
>
> Jesus said to him, 'Receive your sight; your faith has healed you.' Immediately he received his sight and followed Jesus, praising God (Luke 18:35–43).

Prayer is the practical application of dependence. It is the overflow of weakness, turned upwards to our Father through Christ. It is faith put into action as I realise that I can't do life and ministry on my own. This story of the blind man (named 'Bartimaeus' in Mark 10:46–52) gives us a great picture of a weak man overflowing in prayer. As this blind man comes to Jesus, he has nothing to offer or recommend him. He has been rendered powerless through a disability, and is obviously destitute. The one thing that he does know, though, is how to be needy. As Jesus passes, he sits there not in quiet, meditative silence, but raising his voice, demanding to be heard. Here we have a blind beggar who engages in incessant, annoying, noisy and persevering prayer.

In context, it's an ironic depiction of the disciples' spiritual blindness. Just before this miracle, Jesus had told them (yet again) that he was on his way to the cross, but they just didn't understand (Luke 18:31–34), continuing to show their spiritual blindness. This story of the blind man is clearly a comment on that, highlighting how we need Jesus to open our blind eyes to spiritual truth. Yet, we should be careful not to turn this story into a spiritualised parable. After all, the man really did cry out to Jesus in his suffering, and he really was blind. Here was a man who had a real need and whose only help was Jesus.

In my congregation, we have a time in our service when people get to share their needs for prayer. More often than not, the needs that are presented are pretty ordinary and revolve around practical challenges and sicknesses. As pastors, we want people to have spiritual priorities in our prayers, and yet we need to be very careful that we don't too quickly judge the sharing of practical needs. The Lord stoops down to hear the needs of the vulnerable, sick and afflicted. He cares about his people's problems. We mustn't be so spiritual that we're no longer depending on the Lord for daily bread and help in difficulties! Paul Miller tells a great story about his mother that illustrates this truth:

> I recently read an otherwise excellent book on prayer in which the author implied we shouldn't pray for trivial things such as parking places. The author said such requests seem selfish. When I read this, I couldn't wait to tell my mom, Rose Marie Miller … Mom, now eighty-two, works full time as a missionary in London … We met for breakfast, and when I told her what this author thought about prayers for parking spaces, she looked a little incredulous, cocked her head, started laughing, and said, 'How else would you find a parking place? When I am driving with the grandchildren in London, they always say, "Grandma, would you pray that we'd find a parking spot?"'[3]

Just as the blind man's suffering drove his prayer, so will personal needs, trials and difficulties drive us to prayer too. Sickness, worries, family crises and people leaving our church all get us on our knees. Sheer desperation will make us pray. Though we may not have prayed in months, when the crisis comes, we'll call upon the Lord. In trials, even unbelievers pray. There's a preacher's story about an atheist out in the woods who is suddenly confronted by a terrifying grizzly bear. In sheer desperation, he cries out in prayer, 'God, if you're there, save me! This bear is going to eat me. Please turn it into a Christian!' To his great surprise, a big ray of light suddenly shines through the clouds on the bear, accompanied by faint, distant angelic singing. The bear immediately falls on its knees in a posture of prayer. The atheist is astounded to see the bear's spiritual transformation. Softly and reverently, the newly born-again bear then begins to pray, 'Lord, for what I'm about to eat, please make me truly thankful …' Atheists might not get the answer that they're looking for, but even they will pray in need. Desperation is the rocket fuel for our prayer life.

In Luke 18, important people are embarrassed by the blind man's need (v. 39). They despise the man's weakness and don't want him to bother Jesus. This smelly vagrant had, in their view, become a nuisance, and they assume that Rabbi Jesus wouldn't be interested in such a low-life. The man, however, is shameless and unbothered about bothering Jesus. He simply doesn't care what the disciples or anyone else thinks. So, he just shouts louder.

This beggar knows how to pray and how to be blessed. He teaches us that prayer isn't about talking very quietly to the Lord, under our breath, in a dimly lit room and while we sit in a comfy chair. Rather, prayer can be just as much about shouting and demanding the Lord's intervention on a dusty, public street. There's a directness and straightforwardness here that we can learn much from. The man has no power, status or wealth, but knows how to stop the Christ in his tracks: 'Jesus stopped and ordered the man to be brought to him' (v. 40).

Jesus' response to this blind man is also a huge encouragement for our praying. It's clear that, while some are embarrassed by the beggar, Jesus isn't. He doesn't despise him, nor does he ask the man to be quiet. On the contrary, it seems that Jesus loves to be stopped by such requests, and he even condescends to ask the man what he needs. Our dependence gets the Lord's attention and, ultimately, the Lord's blessing. He gives grace and power to the humble.

If there is anything that ministry thrives on, it is needy prayer. In all our struggles, we can know that the Lord loves to be 'stopped' by our prayers. We mustn't be afraid to be bold and opportune in our asking because the power of the Lord is channelled through needy prayers.

Dependent sinners

> To some who were confident of their own righteousness and looked down on everyone else, Jesus told this parable: 'Two men went up to the temple to pray, one a Pharisee and the other a tax collector. The Pharisee stood by himself and prayed: "God, I thank you that I am not like other people – robbers, evildoers, adulterers – or even like this tax collector. I fast twice a week and give a tenth of all I get."
>
> 'But the tax collector stood at a distance. He would not even look up to heaven, but beat his breast and said, "God, have mercy on me, a sinner."
>
> 'I tell you that this man, rather than the other, went home justified before God. For all those

> who exalt themselves will be humbled, and those who humble themselves will be exalted' (Luke 18:9–14).

> One of the criminals who hung there hurled insults at him: 'Aren't you the Messiah? Save yourself and us!'
>
> But the other criminal rebuked him. 'Don't you fear God,' he said, 'since you are under the same sentence? We are punished justly, for we are getting what our deeds deserve. But this man has done nothing wrong.'
>
> Then he said, 'Jesus, remember me when you come into your kingdom.'
>
> Jesus answered him, 'Truly I tell you, today you will be with me in paradise' (Luke 23:39–43).

Thankfully and mercifully, Scripture is full of the prayers of sinners. Where would we be without them? The reality of sin points us to our greatest need and our greatest weakness. Spiritual leaders never get beyond the basic reality of sin in our own lives. We always remain humbled, broken sinners seeking a holy and gracious God. Nevertheless, we can find ourselves easily retreating from this truth. I vividly remember talking to a local church leader who said that, while their church had a very clear and biblical view of sin, he had never heard anyone in his church actually confess a specific sin. They had times of general confession, but it seemed that this had not drilled its way down into their hearts. It's so easy for us to think of ourselves as theoretical sinners, confessing our sin in general ways, without ever confessing any actual real-life sins!

In Luke 18:9–14, we have the well-known parable of the Pharisee and the tax collector. Jesus makes it clear that the tax collector is our model. He is the one who obviously feels inadequate before God, not even looking up, but beating his breast and confessing. This is a man who prays out of a huge sense of spiritual need and who humbles himself in repentance. It's not the capable, gifted and proud Pharisee who approaches God rightly here, but the humbled sinner. We can't come to God via our gifts or our ministry prowess, but only through gospel-driven, sin-acknowledging dependence. If we're to resist the dangers of hypocrisy, public pretence and religious play-acting, we need to keep ourselves as humbled sinners before the Lord. J. C. Ryle wrote of John Bradford, an English reformer and martyr:

> He did not count himself to have prayed to his contentment unless in it he had felt inwardly some smiting of the heart for sin, and some healing of that wound by faith, feeling the saving health of Christ, with some change of mind into detestation of sin, and love of obeying the good will of God.[4]

This kind of mindset, when rightly centred on Jesus, doesn't lead us into continual navel-gazing or introspection, but will shape our leadership character for good. As John Newton says:

> Whoever is truly humbled – will not be easily angry, nor harsh or critical of others. He will be compassionate and tender to the infirmities of his fellow-sinners, knowing that if there is a difference – it is grace alone which has made it! He knows that he has the seeds of every evil in his own heart. And under all trials and afflictions – he will look to the hand of the Lord, and lay his mouth in the dust, acknowledging that he suffers much less than his iniquities have deserved.[5]

An unsympathetic pastor produces anxiety and hypocrisy in people around them, but a deeper sense of our own sin will help us to come alongside others in humility and sympathy. Our critical edge and harshness will be softened, we will preach more gently and we will more easily persevere with others. Above all, mercy will characterise our dealings with fellow sinners. All of this is showing us that leaders need a real conviction of sin's presence in specific ways in their own life if they are to be spiritually effective with others. An authentic Christian character is broken-hearted, shaped by a sense of my deep need of the Saviour.

There is probably no starker picture of the sinner's utter dependence on the Lord than the thief on the cross in Luke 23:39–43. This favourite text of every preacher is obviously a wonderful example of how we're saved apart from anything that we do. Here we have a death-row criminal, obviously a sinner, who is being executed 'justly' (v. 41). There is no possibility of good works saving this man as he is utterly lost. He only meets Jesus as he gasps his own last few breaths. But his encounter with Jesus is an amazing picture of the power of redemption for the least likely of people.

There is more, though, to this man. He's not simply an example of redemption for the worst of sinners; he's also a model of faith. In its context, his faith is extraordinary as he is the only one (apart from the centurion) who responds rightly to the crucified Jesus. In verse 40, the thief rebukes the other criminal: 'Don't you fear God,' he said, 'since you are under the same sentence?' The original word used for 'sentence' here (which means 'judgment' or 'condemnation') is the same one used in 20:46–47 to describe the 'sentence' hanging over the religious leaders. Ironically, the thief knows that judgment is hanging over him while the spiritual leaders don't. The priests are the very ones who have condemned Jesus, with the crowd mocking and despising him (v. 35). The thief, on the other hand, can look at the tortured, despised man next to him on a cross and see both Jesus' righteousness (v. 41) and his kingly rule (v. 42). He has eyes to see what no one else, including Jesus' own disciples, can see. The thief grasps that the Christ must go to the cross. Like the tax collector, he has spiritual wisdom that everyone else around him lacks. His dependence on the cross of Jesus, then, isn't simply as an example of some kind of last-minute reprieve, but displays a unique, exemplary, cross-exalting faith.

We must learn from this not to treat the cross as the ABC of discipleship, but as our A–Z. The cross isn't something that we graduate from as we move onto bigger and better things like preaching and church planting, but it is the centre into which we must go deeper and deeper. A cross-less Christianity is a terrible curse, and a ministry bereft of the crucified Christ will have nothing to offer. On the other hand, the thief on the cross teaches us the wisdom of a cross-centred faith. Such a faith will enable us to lead out of fullness, rest and security. We will minister depending not on ourselves, but on the One who justifies us. Such dependence will rest on God being for us in Christ, whatever else is against us. Thus all leadership has to be shaped by the crucified Christ. He is the lens through which we look at everything in ministry. We are never more than dependent sinners running to, and resting in, his death for sinners like us.

The dependent Son

Finally, there is probably no bigger rebuke to our tendencies towards independence than the life of Jesus himself. It's clear from the Gospels that the Son's relationship to the Father is all about dependence. We see, for example, that he has a throne only because the Father gives it to him:

> The Lord God will give him the throne of his father David (Luke 1:32).

He possesses all things as the Father's gift to him:

> All things have been committed to me by my Father (Luke 10:22).

We see his dependence at Gethsemane:

> Father, if you are willing, take this cup from me; yet not my will, but yours be done (Luke 22:42).

We see his dependence at his death:

> Father, into your hands I commit my spirit (Luke 23:46).

Simply put, we're told that the Son lives under his Father's rule and direction in all things. He does nothing without his Father. This is made very explicit in John's Gospel:

> Very truly I tell you, the Son can do nothing by himself; he can do only what he sees his Father doing, because whatever the Father does the Son also does (John 5:19).

The extraordinary thing here is that Jesus has an absolute and total dependence, as the Son, on his Father in all things. It is true to say that the incarnate Son is the most dependent person in the whole Bible. And, through this, he is showing us that true, perfect humanity looks like dependence. Thus his reliance upon the Father isn't something that he needs to escape, but it is part of his glory and righteousness.

Should we, as leaders, ever expect to be less dependent than Jesus?! Surely, there is nothing more humbling for us than the humility of Jesus, and nothing that exposes our self-sufficiency more than the self-emptying of the Son. Maturity into Christ-likeness must, then, mean a deeper dependence and reliance. As we are united to Christ, and transformed by his life in us, we will be learning to lean harder on the only One who can give us all that we need. This is the path to true power and greatness.

– 4 –

Feeding on Jesus

We live in a world full of groaning (Rom. 8:22). You don't have to live long, nor be in ministry very long, before you understand that this world is a difficult place to live in and has many heartaches. We don't escape this as leaders, facing the same everyday struggles, sorrows, grief and worries as the people we lead. Spiritual leaders, as much as anyone else, can be broken, and twisted up, by life's difficulties. Discouragements, death and dysfunctional relationships impact us as well. While some believers may think that their leaders skirt around those things with consummate ease, we know that we're down in the muck with everyone else. We are all wandering in the wilderness of this world together.

The extra challenge for leaders, though, is that we have to lead everyone else in the middle of this mess. We have a spiritual responsibility for others even while we are struggling ourselves. Our peculiar test is to minister to people when our own hearts are starting to become embattled and embittered by discouragements.[1] But there is both an opportunity and a temptation for us. The temptation is to put on a front, say the right things and make a good show. We can pretend to have a spiritual vitality that we don't. On the other hand, the opportunity is to let this experience send us back to Jesus for fresh supplies of power and spiritual food, and then speak out of that. In other words, we can give into the temptation to become spiritual hypocrites, or we can seize the opportunity for spiritual growth. We can either move further away from the Lord in pretence, or we can go deeper into the Lord's presence.

John 6 is an invitation to come and get what we need from Jesus. Here hungry, empty souls are invited to get living bread to sustain them in their wilderness wandering.

The abundant Jesus

> Some time after this, Jesus crossed to the far shore of the Sea of Galilee (that is, the Sea of Tiberias), and a great crowd of people followed him because they saw the signs he had performed by healing those who were ill. Then Jesus went up on a mountainside and sat down with his disciples. The Jewish Passover Festival was near.
>
> When Jesus looked up and saw a great crowd coming towards him, he said to Philip, 'Where shall we buy bread for these people to

eat?' He asked this only to test him, for he already had in mind what he was going to do.

Philip answered him, 'It would take more than half a year's wages to buy enough bread for each one to have a bite!'

Another of his disciples, Andrew, Simon Peter's brother, spoke up, 'Here is a boy with five small barley loaves and two small fish, but how far will they go among so many?'

Jesus said, 'Make the people sit down.' There was plenty of grass in that place, and they sat down (about five thousand men were there). Jesus then took the loaves, gave thanks, and distributed to those who were seated as much as they wanted. He did the same with the fish.

When they had all had enough to eat, he said to his disciples, 'Gather the pieces that are left over. Let nothing be wasted.' So they gathered them and filled twelve baskets with the pieces of the five barley loaves left over by those who had eaten.

After the people saw the sign Jesus performed, they began to say, 'Surely this is the Prophet who is to come into the world.' Jesus, knowing that they intended to come and make him king by force, withdrew again to a mountain by himself ...

When they found him on the other side of the lake, they asked him, 'Rabbi, when did you get here?'

> Jesus answered, 'Very truly I tell you, you are looking for me, not because you saw the signs I performed but because you ate the loaves and had your fill. Do not work for food that spoils, but for food that endures to eternal life, which the Son of Man will give you. For on him God the Father has placed his seal of approval.'
>
> Then they asked him, 'What must we do to do the works God requires?'
>
> Jesus answered, 'The work of God is this: to believe in the one he has sent.'
>
> So they asked him, 'What sign then will you give that we may see it and believe you? What will you do? Our ancestors ate the manna in the wilderness; as it is written: "He gave them bread from heaven to eat."'
>
> Jesus said to them, 'Very truly I tell you, it is not Moses who has given you the bread from heaven, but it is my Father who gives you the true bread from heaven. For the bread of God is the bread that comes down from heaven and gives life to the world' (John 6:1–15, 25–33).

As we read John 6, we should remember that it is set in a hand-to-mouth world. This wasn't a time of modern agriculture, plenty and abundance, but a time of food shortages and famines. It's hard for us to really know what that felt like. The Covid pandemic, in its early stages, brought a sense of panic to coddled, protected westerners as we obsessed about the disappearance of toilet rolls and hand gels. Panic buying reigned as we became terrified of what might be a shortage. Yet, there never was any real shortage of necessities because we live in material abundance. The world of John 6 was very different. It really was a fragile and needy world, where life was a struggle for the necessities. Jesus' feeding miracle is, then, a spectacular demonstration of how Jesus brings abundance to a destitute, needy people.

In many ways, this sign has the look of an 'accidental' miracle. It seems, on the face of it, unplanned and simply a reaction to a persistent, pursuing crowd. But, in God's world, there are no accidents, and Jesus knows exactly what he is doing. In verses 5–6, it is clear that he had already planned to perform one of his signs to show his glory to the world. In particular, this sign would highlight how Jesus was greater than Moses and brought better manna than what had been given in Israel's wilderness wanderings (v. 32; cf. Ex. 16:1–36; John 1:17). Again and again, the Gospel of John stresses the superiority of Jesus to the old covenant and all of its forms and blessings. We see here that the true Shepherd and Provider has come into the wilderness for his people to bring them into true Passover freedom (v. 4).

In this scene, we find ourselves in the wilderness, with a huge, hungry crowd and no food. Philip is, understandably, incredulous in the face of the overwhelming need

(v. 7). Dealing with it is, on the face of it, an economic (and practical) impossibility. Yet, as always, Jesus ignores the impossibility of it all, and makes the people sit down before initiating the dishing out of a handful of bread and fish. The result is that thousands are fed.

Notice first that Jesus uses what the people already have. He chooses to do a miracle with a few loaves and fish, rather than simply creating food out of nothing. Jesus is the Creator God who sustains every living thing: 'The Son is the radiance of God's glory and the exact representation of his being, sustaining all things by his powerful word' (Heb. 1:3). He could obviously have supplied everyone's need simply by creating a ready-packaged meal for each person. Yet, Jesus takes what they have (John 6:9) and multiplies it beyond anything they could have imagined.

Be encouraged by this if you feel that your ministry is poor and under-resourced. We often think that for anything powerful to happen we first need the Lord to load us up with all the necessary gifts and resources. However, he may well prefer to leave us poorly gifted and resourced, instead supplying our needs by multiplying our 'five loaves and two fish'. We look at what we have and feel that it isn't enough to feed a crowd, but Jesus doesn't have any such worries. What we need is not a plethora of resources, but the hands and blessing of Jesus. He takes what we have and does wonders with it.

Notice secondly how everyone is satisfied: 'they had all had enough to eat' (v. 12). The crowd is not on hunger rations, eating half a sandwich each and trying to make the food stretch for everyone. Not only does everyone get what they need but there are even leftovers – twelve basketfuls (vv. 12–13)! They actually end up with more bread than they had at the start. Jesus' power overflows in abundant provision and good gifts for his people in the wilderness.

My wife is well known in our family for her overestimation of portions. She has an in-built fear that there won't be enough for everyone. I once ate fish pie, originally made for our church, for months after a particularly zealous weekend of cooking. Jesus is not unlike my wife in this regard! When he is at work, he not only feeds thousands but makes more than could ever be eaten. His infinite resources overflow into a surplus supply for all our needs. The encouragement here is that we won't ever be able to out-ask Jesus or out-demand him. We won't leave Jesus exhausted and saying, 'Well, I tried to help you, supply you and fill you up, but you are just too much!' Our emptiness and need are never too big for him. Rather than being called to live our lives and ministries on meagre rations, we have been abundantly supplied with more-than-we-could-ever-use blessings.

Food that spoils

In the miracle of John 6, Jesus has just made food for thousands of people. The crowd, though, has a very limited faith response to Jesus himself. As is common in John's Gospel (see, for example, 3:4 and 4:15), they are only able to grasp this miracle as physical provision, and lack understanding of its spiritual significance. They only see food, and not the meaning behind it.

To be fair, the people are excited and think that Jesus is amazing. Moreover, they recognise that he is some kind of prophet (v. 14). Yet, this still leads them to the wrong response, as they now look to revolt and install Jesus as king (v. 15). They envisage that the Christ will establish a new, greater Israel, liberated from Roman control. This, though, is not Jesus' plan – and he certainly doesn't need help from the crowd. Accordingly, he deliberately 'loses' them. Rather stubbornly, the crowd pursues him once more and find him on the other side of the lake (v. 24). This time, Jesus gives them a rather frosty welcome. It's ironic how unenthusiastic he is in the face of drawing crowds and popularity. In fact, he's more concerned to correct them than receive acclaim in verses 26–27.

It becomes apparent that the people are coming to Jesus for more food – effectively treating him as a walking, talking, miraculous food bank! But Jesus says, 'Do not work for food that spoils' (v. 27). The essence of Jesus' message is, 'Don't make food the main thing you want. Don't make your life about this.' While these people might have had many struggles, and may not always have had food on the table, Jesus tells them that what they need isn't the 'food that spoils'. The people may well have thought, 'Couldn't Jesus now bring an end to world hunger and alleviate poverty with a few more miracles?'! But Jesus' focus is on their need for the true spiritual food that only he brings. He's performed a miracle to feed their stomachs, but he's really come to feed their souls.

We should, though, guard ourselves against misunderstanding this. Some might want to argue from this passage that we shouldn't concern ourselves with social injustices, poverty and hunger. After all, isn't Jesus here pointing the crowd to their spiritual priorities? Yet, that would be a very narrow reading of this passage, and would also neglect the Bible's overall concern for justice and mercy for the poor and vulnerable. Further, it is very clear that Jesus did care about the crowd's bodies, otherwise he wouldn't have already performed a feeding miracle! Therefore, Jesus' words here shouldn't be used to marginalise practical compassion and care for the weak.

Jesus is simply reminding us that everything in this world is 'food that spoils'. All things have a sell-by date. In time, they break, fade and go mouldy. Every achievement is eclipsed. Every possession becomes obsolete. Your iPhone is good for a couple of years but soon looks clunky. Those smart trousers you bought quickly go out of fashion. You save up for something and buy it, yet the joy of the new purchase soon dissipates.

We too will fade. Our hearts aren't atomic clocks that are wound up once and keep on going. Instead, we are winding down. At some point, our health will break down, and our body will turn against us. Death may also come suddenly and unexpectedly. Apparently, more people die from donkeys than in aeroplane crashes, and more people die from coconuts than sharks. Even more striking, deaths due to doctors' negligence are five times the number of deaths caused by firearms! Alternatively, death may come slowly through a gradual decline. There may come a time when we're no longer able to look after ourselves, and have to move into care and then finally into hospital for our last few days. We are food that spoils, aren't we?

> I denied myself nothing my eyes desired;
> I refused my heart no pleasure.
> My heart took delight in all my labour,
> and this was the reward for all my toil.
> Yet when I surveyed all that my hands had done
> and what I had toiled to achieve,
> everything was meaningless, a chasing after
> the wind;
> nothing was gained under the sun
> (Ecc. 2:10–11).

In 2010, an eccentric, eighty-nine-year-old lady, who lived in Torquay and who liked to feed cats, died alone. She had never married and she had never had kids. Sadly, her body lay a few days undiscovered in her flat. The lady's name was Eileen Nearne. We probably have never heard of her; her death was not headline news. Yet, her life story was an amazing one. She and her sister had been secret agents with the SOE (Special Operations Executive, now MI6) during World War II. She secretly entered occupied France in 1942, when she was only twenty-one, and ended up helping to support and run French underground resistance networks for two years. She was then caught by the Gestapo in 1944, horribly tortured and put into a concentration camp. This was, by any standard, a remarkable woman. She made amazing sacrifices and lived an incredible life, but she died forgotten, alone with her cats. Whatever incredible things we have achieved with our lives, the reality is that it all fades. We all decay and disappear. Do we remember the first names of our great-grandparents? Do we know where they are buried? In a hundred years, we too will all be forgotten and our successes will be left behind. At the end of the day, it is all food that spoils.

This should sober us, as leaders are as prone to worldliness as anyone else. Middle age, in particular, can bring a creeping desire for comfort and ease. We can seek to medicate our sadnesses and frustrations in ministry with the things of this world, and distract ourselves from difficulties with little diversions. But Paul warns Timothy, 'No one serving as a soldier gets entangled in civilian affairs, but rather tries to please his commanding officer' (2 Tim. 2:4). People in ministry mustn't become entangled in 'civilian affairs'. This is not a reference here to wickedness or sin, but to the ordinary, everyday, good things of this world. Paul's point is that we have been set apart for ministry, and that should bring a focus to our decision-making and priorities. Spiritual leaders should be wary of being distracted from their calling, even by good, legitimate things. This is not a repudiation of using God's good gifts in creation, nor is it saying that we shouldn't enjoy recreation or rest. It is, however, an exhortation to remember we have been called to 'military service'. The devil can just as easily destroy our ministry through distraction as through temptation. So, ministers should beware an unhelpful focus on the things of this world – even when those are good gifts – because, ultimately, they are food that spoils. Jesus calls us away from a life where we give our energy and effort over to things that fade. He calls us instead to make our lives about something that is solid and lasting.

Food that endures

In Greenland, there is a food type called *kiviaq*. The dish is made by shoving loads of dead sea birds into a seal carcass, which is then sewn up and stored under rocks. Apparently, over time, the birds liquefy and melt into a fine gooey paste. Unsurprisingly, *kiviaq* is pretty smelly – so smelly that you can't eat it indoors – but actually stays edible for up to a year. Of course, the problem is whether or not anyone would ever want to eat anything so disgusting in the first place. Preservation and longevity isn't everything!

Jesus offers us here a food that lasts even longer than *kiviaq*, and which, thankfully, tastes much, much better (John 6:27). Obviously, he is looking beyond our stomachs, and the things of this world, to our souls and our deepest spiritual needs. When it comes to everyday food, some people want quality, while others want quantity. But when it comes to the living bread Jesus offers, we don't have to choose. His food has both quantity *and* quality – it is the very life of God himself that endures for ever (v. 35).

In our weariness, confusion and groaning, we can remember that Jesus is the fullness that we so long for. We haven't been left to fend for ourselves in our trials and struggles. We don't have to lie in bed with sheets over our head, just waiting for it all to end. On the contrary, we have a powerful, generous Shepherd who can give us everlasting bread. He can move the resources of heaven and earth to provide for us. He will lead his sheep from the wilderness to green pastures and restore our souls. We will lack nothing with him. When we feel that we are coming to the end of our tether, we can, at the same time, know that Jesus will be holding the other end of the tether and giving us what we need.

The work of God

The key to living according to the fullness of Jesus is understanding what work he has called us to do. Ministry is undoubtedly a call to hard work. We're commanded to labour for God and his church. Our ministry involves effort and striving for the gospel (Col. 1:29). Yet, behind all that work, there is actually a much deeper work that leaders need to be doing; without it, all the other work won't be worth anything. Jesus describes the deeper work in John 6:29: 'The work of God is this: to believe in the one he has sent.' The essence of this vital work isn't all the ministry activity we're regularly involved with, but to believe in the Son. Believing is the heart and source of all true work. I know that this might all sound a bit unproductive and easy-going for Type A personalities. After all, aren't we meant to achieve something?! As Proverbs 13:4 says, 'A sluggard's appetite is never filled, but the desires of the diligent are fully satisfied.' Jesus, though, tells us that the visible work of ministry needs to begin with the deeper, hidden work of faith in the Son. This is how we get the food that endures. Trying to work for God without that primary work is to look for the food that spoils. It is also a fast route to burnout. There are many reasons why we might burn out, yet we should consider whether we have been working without faith. The nourishment that can sustain us long-term will only come through the means of faith in Jesus.

Faith unites us to Jesus, and with him, we get endless benefits. John Calvin wrote:

> We see that our whole salvation and all its parts are comprehended in Christ. We should therefore take care not to derive the least portion of it from anywhere else. If we seek salvation, we are taught by the very name of Jesus that it is 'of him.' If we seek any other gifts of the Spirit, they will be found in his anointing. If we seek strength, it lies in his dominion; if purity, in his conception; if gentleness, it appears in his birth. For by his birth he was made like us in all respects that he might learn to feel our pain. If

> we seek redemption, it lies in his passion; if acquittal, in his condemnation; if remission of the curse, in his cross; if satisfaction, in his sacrifice; if purification, in his blood; if reconciliation, in his descent into hell; if mortification of the flesh, in his tomb; if newness of life, in his resurrection; if immortality, in the same; if inheritance of all blessings, in his Kingdom; if untroubled expectation of judgment, in the power given to him to judge. In short, since rich store of every kind of good abounds in him, let us drink our fill from this fountain, and from no other.[2]

This faith union with Jesus is pictured in John 6 as eating – as taking hold of him and becoming one with him in the most profound of ways. That was clearly not an easy concept for the people to accept: 'Then the Jews began to argue sharply among themselves, "How can this man give us his flesh to eat?"' (v. 52). Jesus is nonplussed, though. Bread, when digested, goes into our bodies and is united to us, supplying us with its own strength and life. Jesus is this bread for us, and it's hard to think of any closer union than food with a body. It shows us that communion with him is the very means of our being sustained and energised. This picture of bread and eating becomes even more significant as we consider Jesus' death. When we take the Lord's Supper, we remember that this Bread was finally broken for us. On the cross, he offered himself up and was torn apart that we might be mended. Jesus went empty on the cross that we might get a food that endures.

It is truly amazing that Jesus would condescend so low as to make himself our food. God didn't just send us manna, but became our manna through the Messiah, his own Son. Now he has become for us an endless source of sustaining bread. We haven't been left to fend for ourselves in the wilderness. Hungry pastors, weary women's workers and malnourished leaders can all come to Jesus and find limitless sustenance in the face of the most difficult trials. So, let's not be reticent with getting all that we need for life and ministry. Only a fool would fail to do that. Imagine, for a moment, a parallel feeding miracle, where the crowd turns their nose up at the food and leaves it to rot on the ground. Or imagine a crowd so lazy that they wouldn't even raise the bread and fish to their mouth to eat: 'A sluggard buries his hand in the dish; he will not even bring it back to his mouth!' (Prov. 19:24). How could that ever happen? Why would anyone be so foolish? Let's be wise and come to the living Bread to get all that we need.

The troubles that we could be feeling at the moment in our life and ministry might actually be 'hunger pains' for Jesus. Perhaps we're empty, malnourished and desperate for something to keep us going. If so, let's come and get our fill. Let's make sure that, amidst all the challenges and stresses of life and leadership, we are getting the only food that will sustain us. None of us need go hungry. There will even be leftovers. Jesus Christ has committed himself to be our Bread, and he will supply us abundantly with all we need for ever. Life might be hard now, and there might be much groaning, but Jesus doesn't let his people go hungry. Your struggle can't exhaust his sufficiency.

> Come, all you who are thirsty,
> come to the waters;
> and you who have no money,
> come, buy and eat!
> Come, buy wine and milk
> without money and without cost.
> Why spend money on what is not bread,
> and your labour on what does not satisfy?
> Listen, listen to me, and eat what is good,
> and you will delight in the richest of fare
> (Isa. 55:1–2).

– 5 –

Proclaiming Jesus

Now this was John's testimony when the Jewish leaders in Jerusalem sent priests and Levites to ask him who he was. He did not fail to confess, but confessed freely, 'I am not the Messiah.'

They asked him, 'Then who are you? Are you Elijah?'

He said, 'I am not.'

'Are you the Prophet?'

He answered, 'No.'

Finally they said, 'Who are you? Give us an answer to take back to those who sent us. What do you say about yourself?'

John replied in the words of Isaiah the prophet, 'I am the voice of one calling in the wilderness, "Make straight the way for the Lord."'

Now the Pharisees who had been sent questioned him, 'Why then do you baptise if you are

> not the Messiah, nor Elijah, nor the Prophet?'
>
> 'I baptise with water,' John replied, 'but among you stands one you do not know. He is the one who comes after me, the straps of whose sandals I am not worthy to untie.'
>
> This all happened at Bethany on the other side of the Jordan, where John was baptising (John 1:19–28).

During the Covid pandemic in 2020, governments across the world, in an attempt to manage public health risks, barraged us with a whole range of slogans. 'Be safe, be smart, be kind', was the catchphrase of Dr Tedros Adhanom Ghebreyesus, WHO Director General. In the UK, we were urged, 'Stay alert, control the virus, save lives', and to focus on 'Hands, face, space.' Less catchy was the German message: 'Generate evidence, share knowledge, protect and improve health.' Even worse was the Chinese health mantra: 'Confidence consolidation, mutual assistance, scientific prevention, precise policy implementation'! To be fair, these last slogans might sound better untranslated in the original language (!), but we can surely agree that slogans are meant to be catchy. They work because they are pithy and sum up the essence of something.

What kind of slogan, then, could we use to sum up Christian ministry? What are we really doing as leaders? Here's a suggestion: 'It's all about Jesus.' Ministry is really very simple: it's about exalting the Son of God. He is the focus of our teaching, praying and evangelising. We can have no Christian ministry without him. If we want to see a model of how to live this out, there is much to learn from John the Baptist. His ministry displayed a total and utter focus on Jesus Christ.

Preachers often struggle, though, when they come to the sections about John the Baptist in the Gospels, as he can seem something of an unnecessary detour before telling people about Jesus. However, we shouldn't try to move past John too quickly because he is the bridge between Old and New in the Bible. He is the old covenant hope made flesh. To move past John too quickly in a rush to get to Jesus is to move past the Old Testament. The fact is that we need John for our spiritual health. He has much to teach preachers.

In John 1, it's clear that John the Baptist has become, in his own right, a great spiritual leader. He's God's wilderness prophet, who is Elijah-like and filled with the Spirit. His role is to call a remnant to leave their spiritual Egypt and to follow him out into the wilderness through a new exodus (baptism) into the true promised land (the kingdom of God). To that end, he preaches repentance and the forgiveness of sins. He asks the people to recommit themselves once more to their covenant God. As a result, a revival starts in this unknown, and unimportant, place. Crowds come and are baptised in the Jordan as a picture of a new spiritual beginning.

Who John isn't

John was undoubtedly controversial and raised many questions. The authorities were clearly concerned about him, and wondered what he was up to. Was he dangerous? Was he leading a rebellion against Rome? Was he going to cause trouble? Was this of God, or not? We read in verse 19 that John was being investigated and sussed out by the religious authorities. Understandably, they wanted to ask him who he was.

John's reply to their question is quite strongly emphasised: 'I am not the Messiah' (v. 20). So, they wonder if John might be some other revered spiritual figure. Elijah? The Prophet? But the answers are always the same: 'No.' What we get here is a big, fat non-confession. John 1:8 has already told us, 'He himself was not the light', and when we actually get to meet John the Baptist in verses 19–21, we only get more denials. The questions don't yield much information, and so it doesn't seem like anyone is learning much about John! Frankly, it's all a bit disappointing and unexciting for the investigators – what are they supposed to say when they get home?!

The fact is that John has no messianic pretensions. Yes, he's leading a revival and turning the world upside down such that major leaders are taking notice of him (cf. Mark 6:14ff). Yet, his initial concern is to tell them not who he is, but who he isn't. John's self-forgetful non-confession stands in contrast to our contemporary culture. If there is anything that we are interested in, it is who we feel we are. All our kids have been told to reach for the stars and to aspire to be 'somebody'. And we are constantly telling each other on social media that we, and the stuff we have done, is 'amazing' and 'incredible'. This self-preoccupation is older, though, than the twenty-first century and reaches all the way back to Genesis 3. From that moment, we have been reaching not just for the stars but for divinity.

I was talking recently to someone about some frustrations in my life and my failure to trust Christ. My conversation partner gently suggested that the reason that I wasn't depending on Christ was quite simple: I was trying to be the Christ myself! I was immediately convicted as I just hadn't considered what was going on in my heart. It reminded me how easily we drift into messianic pretensions. That thought should make us tremble; this is the very sin of the devil. He is the anti-Christ because he wants to be the Christ. The devil was raised up in the very throne room of God, but fell in pride. Accordingly, Andrew Murray says, 'Pride must die in you, or nothing of heaven can live in you.'[1] Leadership rooted in messianic pretensions, even if it looks like it has been raised up to the heavenlies, will thus subtly be turned towards the purposes of Satan. The devil doesn't need to get us to do anything particularly scandalous. He can just inflame our innate messianic aspirations and watch us become twisted by them.

The very thing that we often hate – the reality of our limitations, failures and weaknesses – is God's mercy to us to remind us that we aren't the Messiah. We so quickly resist and deny these realities, but they are the Spirit's megaphone to us. It's remarkable that John, who was so greatly used by God, so influential and riding on the tide of popular acclaim, could stand so well against the temptations of popularity and celebrity. It seems that part of his resistance to pride came from an understanding of who he wasn't. We need more of John's big, fat non-confession in our lives!

Who John is

In verse 22, the delegation sent to interrogate John are understandably frustrated, and ask him to spill the beans. John is clearly 'somebody', so they need him to say what he is about. This time, John replies more positively: 'John replied in the words of Isaiah the prophet, "I am the voice of one calling in the wilderness, 'Make straight the way for the Lord'"' (v. 23). This famous quote is from Isaiah 40:3, which was originally all about the hope of a new beginning for God's people. God had promised to lead his people out of captivity, through the wilderness, to their homeland. John looks at himself through that Scripture and declares that he is the true herald sent by God. He has, in other words, come as a witness (v. 8). In many ways, John's Gospel is set up a bit like a big trial, with Jesus being the one on trial and John the Baptist as the opening witness for the defence. So, finally, we see why John was so eager to tell us who he wasn't – so that he could tell us who Jesus was. Notice that while Jesus says many times in this Gospel,

'I am ...' John says many times, 'I am not ...' John's 'I am not' means there are no obstacles to us hearing Jesus' 'I am.'

There is, obviously, a big difference between us and John the Baptist; we clearly don't have his ministry. Yet, in another sense, we have something even greater than John. Jesus talks about both these truths in Matthew 11:11. He begins,'Truly I tell you, among those born of women there has not risen anyone greater than John the Baptist ...' According to Jesus, John has an incredibly important role in God's salvation plan. He's more important than all the Old Testament prophets because he's the supreme prophet of Jesus. John brings the clearest, most lucid witness to the Christ. But listen to what Jesus says in the second bit of the verse: '... yet whoever is least in the kingdom of heaven is greater than he.' Astoundingly, Jesus says that the least of his disciples is greater even than John. The point is that just as John was greater than the prophets of the old covenant because of his closeness to Jesus, so we are greater than John because of our relationship with the risen Jesus. John was a witness to the coming of the Messiah on earth, but we know the risen Lord. In other words, we *are* witnesses like John, but we have a ministry that has an even greater status than John's. Ours is a more powerful witness because it is that Jesus is now risen.

We can sometimes feel that our ministries are small, insignificant and marginal – after all, what have we really achieved? Maybe we compare ourselves to the great heroes of the past (or present) who have preached to thousands, written a library of books and initiated world-impacting ministries – all of which makes us feel very unimportant. Yet, however we might evaluate ourselves, we have a greater ministry than Abraham, Moses, Elijah and even John. The prophets dealt with shadows, while we deal with the exalted Lord. They longed for the Messiah's coming (1 Pet. 1:10-11), whereas we speak as people saved in Christ. There is a greatness, glory and significance to what we do because the One of whom we speak is great, glorious and significant. In light of this, it's clear that the privileges of ministry are incredible – as are the responsibilities. We are, therefore, now sent into the world as witnesses. The truth about the Son of God is still under interrogation and we have been summoned to confirm his identity. We've become the voice in the wilderness crying out that he has indeed come, and that he will come again.

The One who comes after

Although John has made clear that he is a witness to the One who is coming, the delegation need more information from him (John 1:24–25). They want to know what kind of spiritual authority he has. After all, he's baptising many and leading a revival. Again, John's answer is very striking because, while the Jewish leaders have made him, and what he is doing, their focus, John himself is looking at Jesus. Where the people see a great spiritual leader baptising in the Jordan, John himself says, '... among you stands one you do not know' (v. 26).

Essentially, John sees himself as just the sideshow. He's nothing more than the warm-up act, or the trailer before the movie. The One who is coming is infinitely greater than the greatest prophet in Israel: 'He is the one who comes after me, the straps of whose sandals I am not worthy to untie' (v. 27). Apparently, a typical disciple of a rabbi or teacher in ancient Israel would have to do anything their teacher asked.[2] There was, though, one exception: changing the master's shoes. Feet were considered the lowest and dirtiest part of the body since they touched the dirty ground. Even today in Middle Eastern culture, showing the soles of your feet is a sign of disrespect. Thus, because feet were considered unclean, changing someone's shoes was the lowest of low jobs, essentially the work of a slave. Yet, notice that John says that he's not worthy even to untie the sandals of the One who is coming. John puts himself even lower than a slave in relation to Jesus. He's not even worthy to be the chattel of his Master. John has an elevated spiritual status, but he sees himself as utterly humbled before the glory of the Christ. He's content to worship in happy self-humiliation at the feet of his Master.

How we need this in our lives! At the heart of so many leadership disasters and scandals is a deep-seated, long-term failure of worship. It is easy for those of us in ministry to work hard without worship being at the heart of what we're doing. Yet, work done without worship is no longer for Christ at all. We can end up being driven more to impact the world than to exalt the worthiness of Christ.

Horizontal priorities of ministry can eat up the vertical priority of delight in him. John, by way of contrast, gives us a taste of heavenly worship on earth by seeing himself as not even worthy to prostrate himself before his Lord. Let's follow him into the throne room and lay down our crowns in self-forgetful, humbled worship.

When your ministry falls apart

> After this, Jesus and his disciples went out into the Judean countryside, where he spent some time with them, and baptised. Now John also was baptising at Aenon near Salim, because there was plenty of water, and people were coming and being baptised. (This was before John was put in prison.) An argument developed between some of John's disciples and a certain Jew over the matter of ceremonial washing. They came to John and said to him, 'Rabbi, that man who was with you on the other side of the Jordan – the one you testified about – look, he is baptising, and everyone is going to him.'
>
> To this John replied, 'A person can receive only what is given them from heaven. You yourselves can testify that I said, "I am not the Messiah but am sent ahead of him." The bride belongs to the bridegroom. The friend who attends the bridegroom waits and listens

> for him, and is full of joy when he hears the bridegroom's voice. That joy is mine, and it is now complete. He must become greater; I must become less (John 3:22–30).

Happiness in ministry easily flourishes when everything is going well and there is growth, but how about when everything seems to fall apart? What do we do then? What kind of people will we be when our life's work seems to evaporate? This is precisely what John, the great revival leader, is facing here. Jesus is clearly surpassing John in influence, crowds and importance. In chapters 2–3, Jesus has already been surpassing purification rituals, the temple and the teachers of the Law, but now even John finds himself eclipsed by Jesus.

John's disciples don't like this development, and complain about this upstart, Jesus, who is taking all the limelight: 'Rabbi, that man who was with you on the other side of the Jordan – the one you testified about – look, he is baptising, and everyone is going to him' (3:26). One can imagine the frustration: 'What's going on here, Pastor John? Jesus is going to put us out of business! He's stealing our sheep! Look, people's lives have been changed, and these disciples have committed themselves. It really isn't OK for someone else to come and steamroller everything!' John's disciples see his ministry as something to be ring-fenced, defended and protected. They want to hoard and hold onto the ministry opportunities they've had.

John, though, knows that everything is a gift of God: 'To this John replied, "A person can receive only what is given them from heaven"' (1:27). Everything he has done, all his influence and every person who has been baptised flows from God's undeserved generosity. John's ministry isn't something that he possesses or owns, but something that he has received. Of course, it's only when something is taken away from us that we truly see our relationship with it. While we give thanks to God for what we have, it is only when it is lost that the genuineness of our gratitude is really made clear. John realises that his ministry isn't his to keep, and that God determines circumstances, situations and blessings. This has a profound impact on his character and convictions: he simply doesn't need to fall apart, personally or spiritually, when his ministry falls apart.

At the heart of John's response is a living faith. He has no envy, fear or insecurity because John actually believes the things that he's been preaching! His own heart has been strengthened by the very word that he has preached to others. So, John tells his disciples, 'You yourselves can testify that I said, "I am not the Messiah but am sent ahead of him"' (v. 28). John reminds them of the message that he has preached consistently and clearly. Wonderfully, John hasn't just said the right things, but has taken them into his heart and lived them out. This is the first job of every preacher and teacher because word ministry will inevitably take us in one of two directions. It will lead us either into absorbing more of God's word into our lives, or into hardening our hearts to God's word. It won't, however, leave us the same. If we teach long enough, we will probably develop both knowledge and skills of communication, yet this isn't the same as a transformed heart. Hearers may initially be fooled by a skilled teacher with a hard heart, but a leader's underlying spiritual reality will sooner or later show itself. Seasons of failure, disappointment or crisis are often those moments of spiritual truth. Let's take care to believe the things we preach – for our own sakes as much as anyone else's.

The bridegroom

Like all good preachers, John uses a vivid illustration to teach his disciples what is going on. This relationship between a bride and bridegroom isn't taken out of thin air, but is deeply rooted in the Old Testament. In that context, it is frequently used as a picture of God's covenantal relationship with his people. According to John, God's people have been betrothed to the Lord Jesus (v. 29). John himself is just a good friend who is present only for the sake of the bridegroom. He waits for the bridegroom to come and be united to his bride, then as soon as the bridegroom turns up, John must fade into the background. The friend isn't centre stage but marginal to the marriage. Essentially, John's disciples want him to nudge the bridegroom out of the way and to pop out a ring for the bride. The bride, though, belongs to the bridegroom and not to John. In a similar way, pastors are only ever the *friends* of their congregations, not the *husband*. The people we lead belong to another: Christ.

Yet, above all, notice how happy John is about the coming of the bridegroom. He is 'full of joy'; he has 'complete' joy. Accordingly, he does not move grumpily to the sidelines or sit down bitterly now that others are turning to Jesus. Rather, John is delighted that the Christ has come. John's heart is given over to Jesus and his happiness is bound up with him. We might gaze in awe and wonder at how easily he can let go of his ministry and give it over to Jesus, but it's because John isn't pursuing something other than Jesus. Rather, he is all about Jesus, and has been since the womb (Luke 1:41). He loves to hear the bridegroom's voice. He doesn't give flat, unbothered, mere assent to truths, but is captivated by and excited about his Lord. Leaders that last have hearts that have been captured by Jesus. Happiness in the Lord and spiritual health go together in ministry.

We have many reasons for joy, but John *specifically* rejoices in the voice of the bridegroom. The word of Jesus brings joy because his presence and his word go hand in hand. Therefore, when Jesus goes to his death, he assures the disciples, 'I have told you this so that my joy may be in you and that your joy may be complete' (John 15:11). His word will mediate to them his personal joy in all its fullness. The voice of the bridegroom is a wonderful thing because it conveys his presence. And that voice, which spoke the world into being and sustains it with mighty power, is our treasure and hope. Scripture is the root of our joy. It will powerfully sustain us and keep us in all trials and disappointments – with joy!

True greatness

John the Baptist has submitted his life to God's purpose and plan: 'He must become greater; I must become less' (3:30). We notice the words 'greater' and 'less' here straight away, but probably the most important word is 'must'. That little word points us to God's sovereign plan being worked out in John's life. The shrinking of John's ministry isn't a result of fate, bad luck or his lack of ability, but of the decree of God. This is why he doesn't push back on it, nor assert himself against it. John accepts God's purpose and subordinates himself to it.

We must be careful that our vision and plans don't take on a life of their own, becoming disconnected from the Lord's purpose. In wanting to take charge of our ministries and lay out a course, the Lord's sovereign purpose can become marginal in our thinking – just like the proud merchants in James:

> Now listen, you who say, 'Today or tomorrow we will go to this or that city, spend a year there, carry on business and make money.' Why, you do not even know what will happen tomorrow. What is your life? You are a mist that appears for a little while and then vanishes (James 4:13–14).

John the Baptist, though, knows that he is a mist here today and gone tomorrow, and that he lives under God's purpose for his Son. We should remind ourselves that proud self-assertion isn't just a sin, but a doomed battle with God. It isn't just wrong, but foolish because it cannot succeed.

God's plan is to exalt Jesus, glorify him and display his greatness to the world (John 17:1, 5). He *must*, therefore, become greater. The Father has planned to boast about his Son, and to show the universe how amazing he is – for ever. This puts everything in our lives in context. As we've already said, John the Baptist is only the trailer for the blockbuster that is about to hit our screens. Once the movie starts, the trailer is unimportant. Accordingly, as Jesus' greatness appears, John must become less.

Our incredible, eternal spiritual privileges as believers come only through Jesus, and they are given to us in such a way that Christ, not us, is glorified as the source. God's plan will always be to exalt his Son. John has absorbed a humility before God in knowing that his leadership isn't for his exaltation, but for Jesus'. Likewise, we mustn't try to become the endpoints of our own ministry. People can't be enamoured by our greatness and Jesus' greatness at the same time. Eventually, one will give way to the other. The motto of every leader needs to be: 'Jesus must become greater; I must become less.' It's all about Jesus in the most ultimate sense possible.

– 6 –

Slaving for Jesus

> Suppose one of you has a servant ploughing or looking after the sheep. Will he say to the servant when he comes in from the field, 'Come along now and sit down to eat'? Won't he rather say, 'Prepare my supper, get yourself ready and wait on me while I eat and drink; after that you may eat and drink'? Will he thank the servant because he did what he was told to do? So you also, when you have done everything you were told to do, should say, 'We are unworthy servants; we have only done our duty' (Luke 17:7–10).

In recent years, many have commented on the fact that we live in the age of 'expressive individualism'.[1] This describes a cultural mindset where personal fulfilment is found through living out what I perceive to be my deepest longings. It's summed up by the slogan, 'We all have to be true to ourselves.' According to this worldview, the job of society and culture is to facilitate the living out of the individual's personal dreams and goals. The basic assumption is that we should all enjoy the freedom to be our authentic selves and find our own inner greatness. This has inevitably turned us in on ourselves as we look inside to find out who we really are. We tend to think that personal autonomy, and the removal of constraints, is key to making a happy society. As a consequence, we consider any hindrance to realising these personal ambitions is intrusive and oppressive. Unsurprisingly, this also has impacted the way we view discipleship. Spirituality itself has become increasingly shaped by personal preferences, choice and comfort. Even God himself is viewed as a means to an end, namely the empowering of my own personal projects.

It would be naive to think that spiritual leaders are immune to this culture. For example, our mindset is often framed by personal ambitions, a sense of call and inner drives. We too feel defined by what we enjoy doing, or what makes us feel most fulfilled. Discussion of spiritual leadership is often preoccupied with our gifts and what we feel suits us personally. Indeed, the personal satisfaction quotient in our lives plays an inordinate role in steering our decisions in ministry. Every leader is now a Jedi knight on a quest for self-realisation.

To read this parable is to enter another world to the one of expressive individualism. It is one of the lesser-known parables, but it packs a very strong counter-cultural punch for a leadership culture that can easily promote a form of spiritualised narcissism. Jesus' teaching is so different to how we've been trained to think that we need to listen to it very carefully. He is instructing us not simply in what we should do in ministry, but in the kind of mindset we need. It's worth paying attention to our emotional reactions as we read this parable, as they will tell us something about our attitude to discipleship and leadership.

Slave, not servant

In looking at this parable, it's important to understand a technical point about translation. We may be misled somewhat by the English translation 'servant' because the original Greek word is actually *doulos*, which clearly, and only, describes a slave – as do all the verbs associated with it.[2] There is a similar issue in the translation of the Hebrew word *ebed* in the Old Testament. It seems to have a range of meanings, and is often translated 'servant' in English Bibles, yet it clearly can also mean 'slave'. We see this, for example, in Genesis 39 with the story of how Potiphar's wife unsuccessfully tries to seduce Joseph. The ESV Bible describes Joseph's relationship to the family as a 'servant':

> ... and she told him the same story, saying, 'The Hebrew *servant*, whom you have brought among us, came in to me to laugh at me. But as soon as I lifted up my voice and cried, he left his

> garment beside me and fled out of the house.' As soon as his master heard the words that his wife spoke to him, 'This is the way your *servant* treated me,' his anger was kindled (vv. 17–19, my emphasis).

Joseph, though, is undoubtedly a slave.[3] In verse 1, he has been bought by Potiphar, his master. Prophets in the Old Testament, such as Moses, are often called God's *ebed* in Hebrew. This is normally translated into English as 'servant'. However, as has been mentioned already, the Hebrew word can also mean 'slave'. This becomes clear in Revelation 15:3 when Moses is called (in Greek) God's *doulos*, meaning 'slave'. He's not just a servant, but a slave! Revelation 11:18 describes the Old Testament prophets in the same way. Our final bit of evidence is Paul the apostle himself. He repeatedly refers to himself as a slave of Christ:

> Paul, a servant [but meaning 'slave'] of Christ Jesus, called to be an apostle and set apart for the gospel of God (Rom. 1:1).

> Am I now trying to win the approval of human beings, or of God? Or am I trying to please people? If I were still trying to please people, I would not be a servant [but meaning 'slave'] of Christ (Gal. 1:10).

This image was clearly formative and significant for how Paul understood his own ministry.

The distinction between 'servant' and 'slave' is a significant one, as we'll see below. Obviously, slavery is a shocking picture for us in our day and age, and has many awful resonances. Importantly, we should remember that slavery in the ancient world was not the same institution as the horrendous transatlantic slave trade. Yet, it was still a shocking picture for Jesus to use even in that time, and the theme runs through the whole New Testament.

The significance of the slavery metaphor becomes clear when we consider the difference between a free person and a slave. A free person in the ancient world had rights, could represent themselves legally and their property wasn't subject to seizure. In other words, they could do what they wanted, and live where they wished. The slave's situation, though, was very different from this. The slave lived under the orders of their master, was represented by their master and had no liberty of movement. Essentially, a slave had no independent existence because a slave was a *possession,* and the master's ownership was absolute. Accordingly, slaves were totally dependent and had lost any right to decide for themselves. They belonged to another and were submitted to their will. Both the slave and the fruit of all his labour were owned by the master.

Paul's words in 1 Corinthians 7:22 are striking: 'For the one who was a slave when called to faith in the Lord is the Lord's freed person; similarly, the one who was free when called is Christ's slave.' Given that slavery is used throughout the Bible as a description of discipleship and ministry, Jesus is telling us something very significant about how gospel ministers are to view themselves. We are not in ministry as autonomous, self-directing individuals. On the contrary, our identity is constructed in a completely different way from that of expressive individualism. We are owned by Another and belong to Someone Else. There can be nothing more challenging to our contemporary mindset, and nothing more undermining of narcissism.

An objection

Despite its biblical usage, believers can feel uncomfortable with this idea of slavery, because it seems to obscure our status as adopted children of our Father: 'Yet to all who did receive him, to those who believed in his name, he gave the right to become children of God' (John 1:12). Isn't the whole point of salvation that we have been set free from slavery for sonship?!

> The Spirit you received does not make you slaves, so that you live in fear again; rather, the Spirit you received brought about your adoption to sonship. And by him we cry, '*Abba*, Father' (Rom. 8:15).

> So you are no longer a slave, but God's child; and since you are his child, God has made you also an heir (Gal. 4:7).

These Scriptures clearly tell us that we are no longer slaves, but children of God. However, while this is wonderfully true, we also need to recognise the complexity of the Bible's depiction of slavery. On the one hand, slavery is, as in the passages above, used as a *negative* spiritual picture to describe our bondage to sin or the Law. At other times, though, slavery is used as a *positive* spiritual picture to describe how we should now live as disciples or gospel ministers:

> Don't you know that when you offer yourselves to someone as obedient slaves, you are slaves of the one you obey – whether you are slaves to sin, which leads to death, or to obedience, which leads to righteousness? (Rom. 6:16).

Thus, in the Bible, slavery can have negative or positive associations depending on the context, and ultimately on who the master is. Clearly, Jesus is using the image in a positive way in Luke 17's parable to describe our relationship with him as Master. This doesn't contradict our status as adopted children, but reflects the richness of all that the Bible says about our relationship with God. He is our Father, and that is central to our relationship with him, but he is also our Lord, King, Saviour and Master. Accordingly, Scripture can speak of us as fully adopted children of our Father and also as subjects of our King and slaves of our Master. We must take into account all that the Bible says of our relationship with God, and not marginalise images (such as slavery) that may, at first, seem less acceptable.

We're subordinated to a Master

If we are slaves, then, it must mean that Jesus is the ultimate Slave Owner. In this parable, he obviously pictures himself as the Master. The word translated 'Lord' (*kyrios*) has a range of meanings, but was also used for slave owners. For example, in Ephesians 6:5–9, the exact same word is used to refer to earthly slave owners and to Jesus as Lord. That is actually key to the whole way Paul subtly marginalises the authority and power of the slave owner over their Christian slaves. The point here is simply that when we call Jesus 'Lord', it has a very authoritative meaning. For example, listen to how Jesus describes himself and his disciples as he washes their feet: 'Very truly I tell you, no servant is greater than his master, nor is a messenger greater than the one who sent him' (John 13:16). When we say that Jesus is our Lord, we're therefore saying not just that he has an exalted status and supreme authority, but also that we are his slaves.

That sense of authority and submission goes all through the parable in Luke 17:7–10. The master is supreme and is the one making all the decisions. The slaves don't demand that they live out their dreams and find their true self. Rather, they're to be all about personal service of the master. They're to await his purposes and plans, rather than their own: 'Prepare my supper, get yourself ready and wait on me while I eat and drink; after that you may eat and drink' (v. 8). In other words, we really are Christ's, who possesses us as our Master. We are there to do his bidding, and so the agenda that steers us is his word and command. He has the priority in all things. This is stated most starkly in the call to take up our cross: 'Then he said to them all: "Whoever wants to be my disciple must deny themselves and take up their cross daily and follow me"' (9:23). In considering these words, we should remember that the cross is a slave's death. It is only fit for those in bondage, as such a death is obviously neither comfortable nor easy. So, taking up our cross means going to places and doing things that we would really prefer not to do.

This is a hard pill to swallow because, to be frank, we might enjoy the sense of power of being up front, teaching and leading. We might enjoy people hanging on our words, and would quite like more of that. Some of us long for greater influence and expansive opportunities to use our gifts (as we perceive them!). At the same time, we struggle to do the mundane, ordinary, unexciting and unseen things. Simple service of others feels beneath us, so visiting the old lady or caring for the single mum are annoying burdens that we easily give away to others. We dislike the mundane routines of service and humble practical tasks, and want something innovative, exciting and adventurous. We want to be in the lights and not low down. After all, who wants to be ordinary? Everyone wants to be extraordinary now. Why else might leaders daydream about being history makers, or having people write biographies of their great deeds in years to come?

This, though, might not be your temptation. The reality is that while there are leaders who want to exalt themselves, there are also leaders who want to run away. The thought of taking up our cross may be not so much a challenge to our pride, but rather a source of fear. We find ourselves quaking before the call to serve, and prefer to hide in a hole. The parable of the talents (Matt. 25:14–30) describes the slave who buries their gift in the ground out of terror of a supposedly hard master. At the end of the parable, Jesus ends up judging him as a worthless slave (v. 30). We face the dangers of fear and laziness, as well as pride and self-centredness.

Christian ministry is slave ministry, and neither a platform for our own greatness nor an escape from challenge. The slave doesn't demand that they do what is most enjoyable, nor what is most easy. They simply get on with what the master has given them to do. Sometimes people say, 'I'll do anything for Jesus' until they're actually asked to do something for him. Then they say, 'I'm not doing that!' Yet, as slaves of Christ, we need to be willing to do anything for our Master – even if it doesn't quite chime with our intuitive desires. Of course, we all have our temperaments, inclinations, desires, likes and dislikes, which can easily give us wisdom in how to serve. The Master providentially equips us for the work he has for us. It's fine to have a list of personal preferences – we just mustn't expect that the Lord

Jesus keeps those lists! He doesn't fit his kingdom around us, but expects us to fit around the kingdom. Those preference lists must not become implicit demands in our lives. The slave isn't there to question or negotiate, but to obey. We serve Jesus in whatever task is required of us. In fact, it takes a tremendous amount of maturity to do mundane jobs. Ordinary service requires huge spiritual power.

One specific question we should think through is *where* we serve the Lord. How do we make decisions about where to serve – and for how long? The idea of serving in a little local church for fifty years, preaching the gospel and then going to be with Jesus, might seem to some like a living nightmare. The idea of uprooting family and moving to the other side of the world to reach an unreached people group might also seem absurd. However, we need to listen to Jesus as he calls people to service:

> As they were walking along the road, a man said to him, 'I will follow you wherever you go.' Jesus replied, 'Foxes have dens and birds have nests, but the Son of Man has nowhere to lay his head.'
>
> He said to another man, 'Follow me.'
>
> But he replied, 'Lord, first let me go and bury my father.'
>
> Jesus said to him, 'Let the dead bury their own dead, but you go and proclaim the kingdom of God.'

> Still another said, 'I will follow you, Lord; but first let me go back and say goodbye to my family.'
>
> Jesus replied, 'No one who puts a hand to the plough and looks back is fit for service in the kingdom of God' (Luke 9:57–62).

Notice how Jesus tells the first man that following him might mean that he will never have a home – something even animals have. To the others he states that family ties and connections are all subordinate to his kingdom and priorities. (This was a huge challenge in a Middle Eastern culture where kinship ties defined identity.) In other words, our Master may bless us with wealth and a big house with a scenic view, or he may not. The point is that the Master's priority isn't giving us the standard of living we demand.

Accordingly, it's worth us questioning ourselves when we suddenly feel mysteriously drawn to leafy suburbs and nice areas. We should be suspicious of the wonderful, mystical peace we feel about moving into comfortable surroundings. We need to reach people everywhere, and yet it is normally the underprivileged communities that tend to be under-evangelised. Might it be that we're less slave-oriented in our decisions about where to live than we like to think?

Moreover, leaders in full-time ministry should be wary of careerism. We can easily think of ourselves as positioned on some kind of promotional ladder, whereby we move to take on more and more responsibility in bigger churches or organisations. Yet, why should it be so? Rather than assuming leadership of bigger groups, churches and organisations, why couldn't leaders just move into more needy communities and areas? A pastor could just as well move to a smaller church if there is need. A slave has no problem with such thoughts.

I work in a poorer area in central London, and though it's not really all that deprived, we have our fair share of problems. A few months ago, I went down to the bin room underneath our church, and found that someone (a human!) had defecated in the room. There I was down on my hands and knees clearing up human poo, and I confess that I didn't receive the task gladly, nor did I feel an abundance of humility doing it. This all felt beneath me as a pastor. Yet, on reflection a little while later, I actually appreciated my enforced humiliation. I was learning that I'm not too important to clear up faeces in a bin area! I really am a slave. Where I serve and what I do is in my Master's hands.

We're unworthy

The word 'duty' is almost foreign to the vocabulary of expressive individualism. It can feel like the enemy of everything that is good and wholesome – a straightjacket for the modern self. The Netflix show *The Crown* has been one of the most successful TV series of recent times, and it chronicles the history of the Royal Family in semi-historical terms. It portrays, in particular, the inner dynamic of the relationship between Queen Elizabeth and Princess Margaret, which expresses itself in terms of a conflict between duty and desire, responsibility and relationship, outward conformity and inward authenticity. Though we respect Elizabeth as she is portrayed in the series – as the dutiful queen – she can also seem joyless and cold. Duty doesn't seem much fun.

We need to rehabilitate this term, though, because Jesus expects us to do our duty: 'So you also, when you have done everything you were told to do, should say, "We are unworthy servants; we have only done our duty"' (Luke 17:10). Duty is about the determination to do what is right and appropriate in the situation. It is subordinating myself to authority, as well as looking to the needs of others. It is about fulfilling my obligations and responsibilities. Duty calls me to serve something bigger than myself, and to keep on doing it when the chips are down. A slave is required, according to Jesus, to do his duty. She has been bought by the master and is there to serve.

The notion of duty transforms the way we feel about unpleasant tasks and hard work in ministry. We can, at times, resent having to go the extra mile, or resist what simply needs to be done. Yet, underneath that attitude is pride. It means I see myself as something more than a slave who is there to do my Master's bidding. I can feel like I should have a medal and public praise any time I do anything vaguely difficult. In such circumstances, ministry quickly becomes unhappy and unfulfilling. However, when we're a humbled slave, we don't make a big deal of hard, mundane jobs, seeing them simply as what is required of us. We echo verse 10 by saying, 'We are unworthy slaves.'

The unworthiness of the slave stands in contrast to the utter worthiness of the Master. When we realise who Master Jesus is, we're happy to fall at his feet. We recognise that we're not worthy to untie his sandals (Luke 3:16), so, forgetting our own worth and glory, we take comfort and joy in his glory. Strangely, there's a contentment in this because we've been liberated from having to be something more than what we are. As we've been set free to be his slave and now belong to him, the mundane, boring, unpleasant tasks of ministry, and the hard work it might involve, are no longer something heroic. We're just doing our duty and serving our Master. Just slaving for him is privilege enough.

We have a wonderful Master

The experience of being a slave is utterly dependent on the kind of master you have. If you have a bad master, it is a nightmare. Peter had to counsel believers who endured awful treatment at the hands of abusive slave owners:

> Slaves, in reverent fear of God submit yourselves to your masters, not only to those who are good and considerate, but also to those who are harsh. For it is commendable if someone bears up under the pain of unjust suffering (1 Pet. 2:18–19).

Enduring life with a harsh master required tremendous character and supernatural endurance.

Yet, we should remember that the call to submit to Master Jesus requires no such character because he is a wonderful Owner. With Jesus we find a Master who is endless in patience and overflowing with compassion. Strikingly, he reveals his heart to us in Matthew 11:28–30:

> Come to me, all you who are weary and burdened, and I will give you rest. Take my yoke upon you and learn from me, for I am gentle and humble in heart, and you will find rest for your souls. For my yoke is easy and my burden is light.[4]

What is striking about these verses is that the 'yoke' mentioned in verse 30 is the language of slavery (see, for example, 1 Tim. 6:1). Jesus is, in fact, telling us what it is like to take on his yoke in our lives – that is, to have him as our Master. He shows himself as a gentle, even humble, Owner. We work for him, but the work he gives us is easy and light. Slaving for Jesus is not a life of being exploited, used and abused, but an experience of deep, ongoing rest. This is unlike any kind of slavery the world has ever known. It's a slavery that liberates, heals and restores. We do indeed have a wonderful Master.

However, the reality is even more wonderful than that. Jesus teaches the parable of Luke 17:7–10 while he's on his journey to Jerusalem to die. In other words, this image of slavery is used by a Master who is on his way to die a slave's death:

> ... he made himself nothing
>   by taking the very nature of a servant,
>   being made in human likeness.
> And being found in appearance as a man,
>   he humbled himself
>   by becoming obedient to death –
>   even death on a cross! (Phil. 2:7–8)

Jesus is the Master who took the very nature of a slave for us. He experienced ultimate degradation and humiliation, dying a slave's death, that we might get salvation with him. What an incredible Master! He completely inverts everything we know about the institution of slavery. This Master becomes like his slaves in order to give them everything that he has. He is the gentle, lowly, rest-bringing Master who dies to bring us into his home and pour out every blessing on us. He is the Slave Owner who shares all that he is and all that he has with us.

In the ancient world, the status of a slave was intimately connected to their master's status. As slaves had no independent status, they were absolutely defined by their owner's social position. In other words, they had status by association. For example, the slave of Caesar actually had huge influence and power because of representing Caesar in everything. We too have a status by association – and what a status we have! For the Lord Jesus has inverted the master-slave relationship not just through his own humiliation, but through his exaltation of us with him. He is the Lord who became a slave so that we, who are slaves, might become lords with him (Eph. 2:6; Rev. 3:21). We now find in him an identity and status that both humbles us (we're slaves) and exalts us (we're seated with him on the throne). We have no glory in and of ourselves, but in Jesus we have an ultimate position.

And so we get to enjoy and represent a wonderful Master full of goodness, love and righteousness. We have a Master who will defend us, will supply us with all we need and loves us to the skies. Slaving for him is the highest privilege we could imagine, and in doing that we receive every good thing we could ever seek. Slaving for Jesus is not the destruction of our lives, but its fulfilment. We lose all things in order to gain all things (Luke 9:24; 1 Cor. 3:21–23). Paradoxically, then, serving Jesus is our great joy and glory. It is as we look away from ourselves in ministry, and submit ourselves to his yoke, that we are actually set free to find rest. We no longer need to find an identity because we have already been found in him.

– 7 –

Longing for Jesus

Once, on being asked by the Pharisees when the kingdom of God would come, Jesus replied, 'The coming of the kingdom of God is not something that can be observed, nor will people say, "Here it is," or "There it is," because the kingdom of God is in your midst.'

Then he said to his disciples, 'The time is coming when you will long to see one of the days of the Son of Man, but you will not see it. People will tell you, "There he is!" or "Here he is!" Do not go running off after them. For the Son of Man in his day will be like the lightning, which flashes and lights up the sky from one end to the other. But first he must suffer many things and be rejected by this generation.

'Just as it was in the days of Noah, so also will it be in the days of the Son of Man. People

> were eating, drinking, marrying and being given in marriage up to the day Noah entered the ark. Then the flood came and destroyed them all.
>
> 'It was the same in the days of Lot. People were eating and drinking, buying and selling, planting and building. But the day Lot left Sodom, fire and sulphur rained down from heaven and destroyed them all.
>
> 'It will be just like this on the day the Son of Man is revealed. On that day no one who is on the housetop, with possessions inside, should go down to get them. Likewise, no one in the field should go back for anything. Remember Lot's wife! Whoever tries to keep their life will lose it, and whoever loses their life will preserve it. I tell you, on that night two people will be in one bed; one will be taken and the other left. Two women will be grinding corn together; one will be taken and the other left.'
>
> 'Where, Lord?' they asked.
>
> He replied, 'Where there is a dead body, there the vultures will gather' (Luke 17:20–37).

I want you to imagine a night when you go to bed, fall asleep quickly and effortlessly, and sleep a good eight hours. You wake up in the morning feeling refreshed and full of energy, but, when you open your eyes, you are astounded to find yourself in a place other than your bedroom. You look around and, rather than seeing familiar objects, you are very startled to see blinking lights and strange screens. You get up, walk around and quickly discover that you have woken up on a massive spaceship. You are, of course, extremely confused, wondering what on earth is going on. You gather yourself and, seeing another passenger, run over to them. Trying to quell the rising panic, you ask breathlessly, 'Excuse me, madam, I see that we're on a spaceship. Would you please tell me where this spaceship has come from?'

The lady looks at you kindly, shrugs her shoulders and says, 'Do you know, I've been asking myself that question for some time, but I haven't got the foggiest idea!'

You then look for someone else. Thankfully, there is a young boy stood close to you. You ask him, 'Excuse me, young man, what is this spaceship doing? Why are we here?'

He smiles and replies, 'Dunno. But do you wanna try some of my ice cream?'

Feeling exasperated, you try with one final person, a wise-looking elderly man sat down opposite you. 'Excuse me, sir, where is this spaceship going? What's the destination?'

He is quiet for a moment, and then says calmly, 'Yes, I used to ask myself that question, but I found no answer. It's better not to think of such things.'

Now given this bizarre situation, and the unhelpful responses you've received to your questions, how would you feel? Surely, it would be terrifying! Yet, the spaceship which we're describing is very familiar; it is, in fact, 'Planet Earth'!

This little parable reminds us that, for the vast majority of people, the world is a confusing, meaningless, absurd place – even if they would never express that. They live with no answers to the big questions of life, and thus no real clarity about why we are even here. As believers, we're thankful to know that we don't live on a meaningless spaceship. Rather, Scripture tells us that we live in a world that has been made for the Lord Jesus Christ:

> The Son is the image of the invisible God, the firstborn over all creation. For in him all things were created: things in heaven and on earth, visible and invisible, whether thrones or powers or rulers or authorities; all things have been created through him and for him. He is before all things, and in him all things hold together (Col. 1:15–16).

Jesus is the apex, goal and centrepiece of everything. All things have been made through him and for him. So, with him, we find answers to all our big questions about the meaning of life. This is a tremendous encouragement when we face dark and discouraging days in ministry. Our lives aren't meaningless absurdities heading towards oblivion, nor are we meaninglessly shouting into the void. On the contrary, we exist through a divine purpose and live in light of a great goal: the day when the Lord Jesus will return. Our 'spaceship' is heading towards him.

The return of Jesus is undeniably a central, core aspect of the gospel (see, for example, Matt. 25:1–46; Rom. 2:16; 1 Thes. 1:8–10). We ignore it at our peril because it is the very end towards which all things are heading. It is, then, strange that his return can be so neglected and marginalised in our preaching and thinking. In many of our churches, the return of Christ is hardly ever mentioned, and it therefore has very little impact on the day-to-day living of believers. Why is this? How can we allow ourselves to neglect such an important part of the gospel?

One reason is an understandable reaction to false teaching. We become tired of people heralding the imminent end of the world, and saddened when we see groups follow them. A number of years ago, the American preacher Harold Camping became internationally famous when he predicted the return of Jesus quite specifically. Today you can go on www.raptureready.com where a so-called 'rapture index' draws together all the signs of the end times. According to its own self-description, it is 'a Dow Jones Industrial Average of end-time activity or prophetic speedometer'. We react negatively to such distortions, fanaticism and sensationalism, but in our desire to be reasonable and moderate, we can give the impression that the second coming of Christ is insignificant and unimportant.

However, the issue for us might not be theological. Look at Luke 17:22: 'The time is coming when you will *long* to see one of the days of the Son of Man' (my emphasis). We may not get easily drawn away to feverish apocalyptic fantasies, nor tempted by millenarian conspiracies, but, if we're honest, do we long for Jesus?[1] It's very sobering to think that part of our immunity to these eccentricities isn't just theological rigour nor biblical literacy, but actually a coldness towards Jesus. Obviously, the return of Christ is about Christ, and so it follows logically that our focus on his return reveals something about our focus on him. Our lack of preoccupation with the second coming is actually a lack of preoccupation with Jesus. We are scornful of those who predict Christ's return in great detail, but at least they *want* Jesus to return. If a man's wife went on a trip abroad and he just wasn't bothered whether she returned tomorrow, in six months or in two years, that would surely indicate that there was something worrying about their relationship. The intensity of the longing stands in direct proportion to the intensity of the love. So, to neglect Jesus' return is to neglect him. Do we long for him to return?

According to the New Testament, Christian discipleship is shaped by an intense desire for Jesus to come. Disciples just can't be happy without the personal presence of Jesus. They are full of restlessness and unease because he isn't here. Believers have a separation anxiety – even as they know that they are united to him in love. We believe in him, but don't see him now (1 Pet. 1:8). We're still waiting to be clothed in him (2 Cor. 5:2), so we're now full of groaning (Rom. 8:23). Paul says that 'as long as we are at home in the body we are away from the Lord' (2 Cor. 5:6). We are instructed to regularly pray, 'your kingdom come' (Matt. 6:10). One of the earliest Christian prayers was, 'Come, Lord Jesus' (Rev. 22:20). Disciples should long for the second coming because they want to be in the presence of Christ. The intensity, or absence, of longing we feel will inevitably shape the people we lead. This isn't a side issue because, as we have seen, discipleship in the New Testament is shaped by that horizon of longing. We need to show our communities that the goal of our ministry or local church isn't the church itself, but Jesus.

The King has already come!

In our passage, Jesus himself teaches us about his return. The context is Jesus' ongoing journey to Jerusalem to die (Luke 17:11). On the way, some Pharisees want to put a tough theological question to Jesus about when the kingdom will come (vv. 20–21). However, in asking that question, they fail to see who is stood right in front of them.

A few years ago, my wife and I took our kids to a little, local playground. There is nothing significant about the playground – just a few swings, a slide and a sandpit. A woman was there with her child, replete with bodyguards and a nanny. Now, I had no idea that this was Janet Jackson – until my wife told me. Right in front of me was an international celebrity, known throughout the world and who has sung to thousands, but I had no clue that she was anything special. My wife couldn't believe that I was so ignorant!

Yet, I have to admit that I'm not all that embarrassed about it. I mean no disrespect to Janet Jackson, but whether or not I recognise her has no real bearing on my life. However, while celebrity awareness doesn't really matter, it really *does* matter whether or not we recognise Jesus!

In our verses, the Pharisees get it spectacularly wrong. They are asking Jesus all about the kingdom and trying to engage him in theological speculation. Ironically, though, they have no idea that they're actually talking to the King. They want to know about the kingdom, but fail to understand that this is actually the personal reign of the Lord Jesus. They are, as Jesus says, preoccupied with careful observations (looking at raptureready.com?!), but aren't observing what is right in front of their eyes. Signs, omens and indications of the coming kingdom are obscuring their view, not helping it.

Jesus tells them, 'the kingdom of God is in your midst' (v. 21). However, we shouldn't interpret this to mean that the kingdom is something internal to them. After all, the kingdom of God can't be in the Pharisees because they are the very ones opposing Jesus! Further, the New Testament nowhere speaks of the kingdom of God entering people, but rather of people entering the kingdom. The problem for the Pharisees is that they don't see the King who has come in their midst. Jesus is, in effect, saying to them, 'I have come!' In looking for the coming kingdom, the Pharisees have disconnected the kingdom of God from God the King.

It's striking how much this attitude continues today. People talk vaguely about 'kingdom work', when actually what they're doing has very little to do with promoting *King* Jesus. They are doing good works, but without any gospel of Jesus. They are public-spirited, but with no preaching of Jesus. They talk of building the kingdom, but forget that the New Testament says we don't do this. No one can build Jesus' reign; we can only come under it. The kingdom of God is about the Lord Jesus, and that means he has to be the substance of our ministry. Our work must be making our King known.

Yet, it is also striking that Jesus doesn't stop there when speaking to the Pharisees. When he effectively says, 'I'm in your midst', he doesn't mean that the job is done. He's not suggesting that we can all pack up and go home because the 'kingdom of God is in your midst'. No, immediately, Jesus turns his disciples' minds to the future, as he moves from his first coming to earth to his second coming. In other words, to use theological jargon, there is a movement towards consummation. We see here that the first coming of Jesus is future-oriented. He is constantly looking to when he will come back. In all the Gospels, as the cross looms, Jesus speaks much of when he will return. Even as he takes in the suffering ahead, he looks beyond it to the end and final victory. Extraordinarily, as Jesus prepares for the cross, he looks to the future.

This mindset continues all through the New Testament. It is noticeable that the first believers were so future-focused, while we ourselves tend to be nostalgic. We look back wistfully to the good old days when Jesus was on earth. We wonder what it would have been like to see Jesus feed the five thousand or raise Lazarus or heal the sick. We might wish that we too could walk on water with him. Yet, the New Testament believers were looking forwards rather than backwards. They weren't all going on pilgrimages to the holy land to try to recover some golden age in the past. On the contrary, as aliens and strangers in this world, they were looking expectantly and hopefully to his return and judgment: 'Since you call on a Father who judges each person's work impartially, live out your time as foreigners here in reverent fear' (1 Pet. 1:17).

When Jesus will come again

Notice that, in Luke 17:22, there is a change in the people being addressed by Jesus. He is now turning his attention away from the Pharisees to the disciples. Another difference is that Jesus *assumes* that his followers will have an *acute* longing for him. In effect, he is saying, 'I know that you're going to intensely desire for me to come again, but I won't. I know that you are going to feel frustration and impatience.' When we feel under pressure, we can overstress the peace, satisfaction and fulfilment of the Christian life now. Jesus actually seems to be predicting that life will be pretty frustrating. His followers will want something, but won't be able to have it! In verse 23, those followers will face the temptation to short-circuit his coming precisely because of that frustration. They will want to fast-forward to the end, and so we're told some will say, 'There he is!' or 'Here he is!' They will want someone to be the Messiah for them.

There are always individuals who are willing to meet this need. I am old enough to remember the one-time footballer David Icke famously being interviewed live by the chat show host Terry Wogan in the 1980s. Icke claimed to be the Son of God on live TV, and was subsequently publicly mocked, leading him to have a breakdown. The sad reality is that messianic pretenders are fairly unstable people. There is a mental illness known as Jerusalem syndrome, which has been known to Israeli psychiatrists for decades. It shows itself in religious pilgrims to Israel who start to think that they have become biblical figures such as Jesus, John the Baptist or Moses. There are also, of course, the more dangerous examples of infamous cult leaders such as Jim Jones and David Koresh.

Though evangelicals are not the kind of people to get carried away by messianic pretensions, we still face the temptation to short-circuit Jesus' second coming with some kind of revival or reformation. We can think, 'If only we could have some revival like in the past … If only our denomination could be reformed … If only we could fix our preaching … If only we could start a church-planting movement … If only we could convert the government … then everything would flow!' But the reality is that, despite what we think, these things wouldn't bring about a crossing of the Jordan or a tumbling down of Jericho's walls. Revivals always fade and reforms always become corrupted in some measure. I'm not dismissing any of these things, and I pray and hope that we might see them. But the fact is that heaven won't come on earth through some spiritual movement among us. What we really need most isn't revival or reform, but Christ's return. Our first prayer shouldn't be for revival, but to ask, 'Come, Lord Jesus.'

We should remember that, while there will always be doubts about revivals and reformations, there will be *no* doubts about the authenticity of the second coming. There will be no questions such as, 'Wait a minute … is this really Jesus?' for we are told that his coming 'will be like lightning which flashes and lights up the sky from one end to the other' (v. 24). In other words, it will be blindingly obvious and public. My wife's grandma was actually struck by lightning and knocked unconscious. As you can imagine, she lived in terror of thunderstorms for the rest of her life. My wife's mum inherited the fear, and has to hide in thunderstorms. Even my wife has some fear of them. My point is that you know if you've been struck by lightning! You don't say, 'Oh, what was that? Was it a bit of static?' It is utterly unmistakeable. In the same way, when the coming of Jesus lights up the world, there will be no doubts.

Before the disciples get carried away, strap themselves in and assume that the kingdom is about to come in all its fullness, Jesus moves them back to the order of things: 'But first he must suffer many things and be rejected by this generation' (v. 25). As he has already been doing throughout the Gospel of Luke in a series of predictions, Jesus points them to the cross. In this fifth prediction, Jesus reminds Peter that he is on his way to die. While we've already seen that Jesus looks to his consummation as he heads to the cross, he also looks at his consummation *through* the cross. The Lord of Glory and the Suffering Servant are the one and the same. There is an order to the gospel – we can't understand the cross without looking to the second coming, nor can we understand the second coming without going through the cross. If we keep that gospel order, we won't go wrong.

The shock of Jesus' second coming

The return of Christ will be a day of judgment. It will be the Day of the Lord spoken of so much by the Old Testament prophets. It is clear that there will never be any shock greater than this Day, which will overwhelm more than a cancer diagnosis, a pandemic or planes flying into skyscrapers. Though we don't know the date nor hour of Jesus' coming, and much will shock us, in another sense there will be nothing surprising about it at all. We should be expecting this Day because it has already been pre-figured and pre-empted throughout the whole of Scripture.

In verses 26–29, Jesus gives us a biblical theology of judgment, focusing on two particular examples: Noah and Lot. Both the stories, as told by Jesus, follow the same pattern of a sudden change of fortune. Jesus says that, for the people of their time, it seemed that everything would just go on normally as it always did. They were feasting and having fun, marrying and planning a life together, buying and selling property. The original Greek conveys this sense of ongoing activity. As life and celebration were the order of their day, they were unconcerned about God and unprepared for judgment. But, in both cases, the shock of judgment came.

The tense of the verbs shifts in verses 27 and 29 to highlight a specific moment of change. Suddenly, without an air-raid siren, alarm or public announcement, flood and fire are poured out. Whether it's in the middle of the wedding reception, or as the estate agent confirms the offer on the dream house, or as people walk out into their manicured garden on a beautiful summer's afternoon, flood and fire suddenly come. We read the chilling words 'and destroyed them all' (vv. 27, 29). This destruction is abrupt, total and final. Even just reading about it is like having a bucket of ice suddenly poured over us. We're left uncomfortable as everything that is solid seems to melt. Whatever our theological position on the millennium (cf. Rev. 20:1–6), it is certainly the case, in this particular passage, that the church remains a remnant amidst terrifying, holy judgment.

We all know the old cliché that the Old Testament is supposedly all judgment and the New Testament is supposedly all love and grace. These verses clearly expose that as false. Here the New Testament is like the Old Testament in that Jesus uses two of the most shocking examples of judgment in the Old Testament to teach us about the day he will return. These two events were, according to Jesus, not mere aberrations under a harsh old covenant, but patterns for his second coming. And they serve as the horizon for our discipleship and ministry today. The Jesus we long for is the coming Judge.

We need to keep coming back to this horizon of judgment for our ministries. There is no doubt that the ideal is for our ministry to be driven by joy and love for Jesus, a zeal for his glory and a longing for his kingdom. But the reality of life is that zeal wanes and love is drained. We easily drift in ministry. We become distracted by a hobby, binge on Netflix, obsessively tidy our desks and dream of living in a bigger place. In other words, we become spiritually sleepy. Accordingly, this horizon of judgment is a strong cup of coffee for sleepy leaders. It wakes us up. How can we snooze in the middle of fire and flood? How can we daydream when destruction is coming? We need to take another look at the reality of judgment. There is work to be done, people to get onto the ark and neighbours to drag out of Sodom. Jesus' coming will be a shock for the world.

How to prepare for Jesus' second coming

Marcio Gomes was a resident on the twenty-first floor of Grenfell Tower during the infamous fire in 2017. After waiting two hours for help, he defied an emergency call handler's instructions to stay put and ushered his family out of their apartment. He wrapped them in wet towels and they all went down the stairways, stepping over bodies on their way. But when he reached the lower levels, horror struck as he realised his twelve-year-old daughter, Luana, had not made it all the way down. She had been rendered unconscious by the smoke and fumes on the stairwell. What does a father do in that moment? Marcio Gomes left his wife, Andreia, and his other ten-year-old daughter, and ran back into the fire to drag Luana to safety.

That's a scary and heroic thing to do. The council estate I work in used to be run by the same organisation that ran Grenfell Tower and is similarly made up of twenty-storey tower blocks. I cannot imagine the courage and sheer physical demands needed to go back up the tower. However, for a moment, imagine that the story was different. Suppose that Marcio Gomes got to the bottom of the tower and then realised that he'd forgotten his iPhone in his flat. Next, picture him feeling so desperate and overwhelmed by the thought of losing his latest gadget that he runs back in! It's fair to say that our response wouldn't be the same, would it? In that scenario, Marcio wouldn't be seen as a hero, but as a fool.

In the final verses of Luke 17, Jesus is effectively warning us, 'Flood and fire are coming, so don't be fools! Don't run back for what you cannot hope to keep!' He's telling us to leave it all behind. Of course, we still love people (Rom. 13:8), seek to save our hearers (1 Tim. 4:16) and snatch people from the fire (Jude 23). But we mustn't love the world because we mustn't love that which is under judgment. Jesus reminds us of Lot's wife in verse 32. She seemed like a believer and was connected to God's spiritual family. She had actually fled Sodom, and almost escaped. However, as J. C. Ryle says, 'though she fled, she left her heart behind'.[2] She looked back with fondness, nostalgia and affection on that which was going to be destroyed, and so she was destroyed as well.

A love for this world still lives on in the best of us and shows itself in all kinds of ways. For example, we may well find that as soon as the activity of ministry is stopped, for a break or a holiday, a surprising amount of worldliness bubbles to the surface. Suddenly, we find ourselves dreaming of another life, our spiritual disciplines disappear and we fritter away time. Our gospel priorities can ebb away in these times, and so we discover that our ministry is making us appear more spiritual than we really are.

A while back, I went to visit a very nice, friendly guy who worked in Google headquarters in London. He wasn't a believer but we got on well, and he showed me around and was incredibly hospitable. It has to be said that the Google HQ was very impressive and cutting-edge – with free gyms, restaurants and a cafe! In addition, people came to work when they wanted, and there was no dress code! I, a mere pastor of a small congregation on a housing estate, found myself in this formidable place. It was very easy to think, 'Really? What am I doing? What are we compared to this?'

Underneath the surface, we can find ourselves still very much in awe of the world. We haven't actually left it all behind, but are lingering there, like someone wanting to jump off the ark for a swim in the flood waters, or to drive back with Lot's wife to Sodom. The devil doesn't need to turn us into a heretic, as long as he can get us to look back and long for what is going to be destroyed.

This is why we need Jesus' gospel principle: 'Whoever tries to keep their life will lose it, and whoever loses their life will preserve it' (v. 33). There are, according to Jesus, two approaches to the world. On the one hand, we can linger, look back and love our life. Or, on the other hand, we can leave it all behind and lose everything for him. We should be in no doubt that these two approaches to the world lead to a terrible separation on the day of judgment. In verse 34, Jesus speaks of there being two in one bed, but one is taken, while the other is left. In verse 35, he pictures two friends working together, and again, one is taken, but the other is left. It's dramatic and unnerving as we see that judgment separates and divides even the closest relationships. In this world, family and friendships cross spiritual dividing lines. But on the Day of the Lord, there will be absolute clarity. Instead of a vagueness and bridging of that dividing line, there will be an eternal separation and division.

Will we linger and look back at the world, or will we leave it behind and be willing to lose everything for Jesus? Some will be running out of the burning building, while some will be running back for their iPhones. We need to make sure that we're choosing rightly for ourselves. And, again, these future realities should animate and drive our ministries. We are dealing with people's eternal destiny, so these verses should certainly sober us as we seek to preach Christ and make him known. With the building burning down, there is a sense of urgency to what we do. We need intentionality, focus and purposefulness. We long for the return of Jesus, but we long for many to turn to him as well. Let's prepare not just ourselves but others for the sudden coming of the Lord.

– 8 –

Knowing Jesus

So the soldiers took charge of Jesus. Carrying his own cross, he went out to the place of the Skull (which in Aramaic is called Golgotha). There they crucified him, and with him two others – one on each side and Jesus in the middle.

Pilate had a notice prepared and fastened to the cross. It read: **JESUS OF NAZARETH, THE KING OF THE JEWS**. Many of the Jews read this sign, for the place where Jesus was crucified was near the city, and the sign was written in Aramaic, Latin and Greek. The chief priests of the Jews protested to Pilate, 'Do not write "The King of the Jews", but that this man claimed to be king of the Jews.'

Pilate answered, 'What I have written, I have written.'

When the soldiers crucified Jesus, they

took his clothes, dividing them into four shares, one for each of them, with the undergarment remaining. This garment was seamless, woven in one piece from top to bottom.

'Let's not tear it,' they said to one another. 'Let's decide by lot who will get it.'

This happened that the scripture might be fulfilled that said,

'They divided my clothes among them
    and cast lots for my garment.'

So this is what the soldiers did.

Near the cross of Jesus stood his mother, his mother's sister, Mary the wife of Clopas, and Mary Magdalene. When Jesus saw his mother there, and the disciple whom he loved standing near by, he said to her, 'Woman, here is your son,' and to the disciple, 'Here is your mother.' From that time on, this disciple took her into his home.

Later, knowing that everything had now been finished, and so that Scripture would be fulfilled, Jesus said, 'I am thirsty.' A jar of wine vinegar was there, so they soaked a sponge in it, put the sponge on a stalk of the hyssop plant, and lifted it to Jesus' lips. When he had received the drink, Jesus said, 'It is finished.' With that, he bowed his head and gave up his spirit.

> Now it was the day of Preparation, and the next day was to be a special Sabbath. Because the Jewish leaders did not want the bodies left on the crosses during the Sabbath, they asked Pilate to have the legs broken and the bodies taken down. The soldiers therefore came and broke the legs of the first man who had been crucified with Jesus, and then those of the other. But when they came to Jesus and found that he was already dead, they did not break his legs. Instead, one of the soldiers pierced Jesus' side with a spear, bringing a sudden flow of blood and water. The man who saw it has given testimony, and his testimony is true. He knows that he tells the truth, and he testifies so that you also may believe. These things happened so that the scripture would be fulfilled: 'Not one of his bones will be broken,' and, as another scripture says, 'They will look on the one they have pierced' (John 19:16–36).

The Gospel of John could have ended in chapter 18 with Jesus ascending to heaven like Enoch, or like Elijah on his chariot. Jesus could have been wonderfully rescued from his persecutors and taken up to glory. That would have been a very fitting end for someone so important, powerful and holy such as Jesus. That is exactly what Islam preaches – and it makes a lot of spiritual sense to the average person.

But John's Gospel doesn't end like that. It finishes with the cross and resurrection of Jesus. Moreover, John's Gospel, together with the whole of the New Testament, shows us that a true knowledge of Jesus can *only* be had through his cross. We may see his humility in his birth and his power in his miracles, and hear his wisdom in his teaching, but to know him and have fellowship with him can only be through the crucifixion (20:20, 27).

Therefore, John 19 doesn't give us an account of how Jesus, the Prophet, is saved from an awful death, with everyone becoming religious and resolving to do better. On the contrary, the very horror of Jesus' crucifixion demonstrates God's astounding grace to a hard-hearted humanity. John 19 reveals that Christianity isn't a series of steps through which we fix our relationship with God, but is a message of salvation from God. Accordingly, this chapter doesn't raise a problem for believers, but is at the heart of what we confess. Christian preaching is tasked with communicating this message. Authentic ministry is always cross-centred ministry: 'For I resolved to know nothing while I was with you except Jesus Christ and him crucified' (1 Cor. 2:2).

A finished work

Like many churches, we've hosted Alcoholics Anonymous (AA) groups in our church. As a result, our building has regularly been filled on a Saturday with people struggling to get past alcohol and other addictions. The groups have had a big impact on many people's lives – including a few in our congregation.

The Twelve Steps of AA are methodical and, in some ways, quite profound. They're infused with a lot of spirituality and ideas about God:

> [We] Came to believe that a Power greater than ourselves could restore us to sanity (Step 2).

They involve a deep self-searching, which pushes people to really see who they are:

> [We] Made a searching and fearless moral inventory of ourselves (Step 4).

They also enforce a changed mindset as well as a process of making amends to people around you for the things you have done:

> [We] Made a list of all persons we had harmed, and became willing to make amends to them all (Step 8).

It's clear that, through a series of specific soul-searching steps, AA has had a deep impact on many people's lives and enabled them to get free from their addictions.

Yet, while alcoholics might be changed by the Twelve Steps – and other people might be changed by finding new resolutions in their lives – John 19 shows us that this can't work for our relationship with God. The bedrock of our salvation isn't in anything within us, by way of us resolving to change, but is in the finished work of Jesus alone. The gospel isn't 'new resolutions for a new year', but Christ crucified. No matter how deep or how profound it is, our resolve to change will never be enough.

There's a folk story about a dad who wants to teach his son right and wrong.[1] He gets a block of wood, then every time his son does something wrong, the dad knocks a nail into the piece of wood. However, when his son improves and changes, the dad removes a nail. This is how many people think of the Christian life: it's about removing nails. The problem, though, is that the holes remain in the wood, even when we've removed the nails. We can't fix our relationship with God by anything that we do because the holes go too deep. We're simply too corrupted and too damaged. Accordingly, we don't preach 'turn to God and sort yourself out', but the finished work of Christ.

John 19, then, is all about this finished, completed work. Earlier, in John 4:34, Jesus says this: 'My food … is to do the will of him who sent me and to finish his work.' In other words, Jesus lived to *finish* his Father's purposes, and the cross is the completion of that work. Finishing or fulfilling[2] is mentioned three times in 19:28–30:

> Later, knowing that everything had now been *finished*, and so that Scripture would be *fulfilled*, Jesus said, 'I am thirsty.' A jar of wine

> vinegar was there, so they soaked a sponge in it, put the sponge on a stalk of the hyssop plant, and lifted it to Jesus' lips. When he had received the drink, Jesus said, 'It is *finished.*' With that, he bowed his head and gave up his spirit (my emphasis).

The death of Jesus on the cross wasn't simply the end of a good life, but was the completion of a task. It was the fulfilment of God's plan to save a people for himself. That is why, in the Gospel of John, the closer we get to the death of Jesus, the more we're told that events are happening in terms of Jesus' work being finished or Scripture being fulfilled (13:18; 17:4, 12, 23; 19:24, 36, 37). The allusions and references to the Old Testament throughout chapter 19 reinforce this:

- Jesus' carrying of the cross (v. 17) reminds us of Isaac, Abraham's beloved son, carrying wood to a place of sacrifice in Genesis 22.
- The famous division of Jesus' clothes (vv. 23–24) reminds us of the righteous sufferer in Psalm 22:18.
- Jesus' declaration that he is thirsty (v. 28) echoes Psalm 22:15.

Notice as well the specific references to the Passover celebration throughout chapters 18–19. In 19:29, there is an allusion to the hyssop plant, which was used to sprinkle blood of the sacrificial lamb on the Israelites' door posts. In verses 31–33, we're told that Jesus' bones weren't broken like the Passover lamb. All this humiliation and degradation is no accident. Jesus is not in the hands of fate or chance, nor has the world spun out of control. On the contrary, the Son is finishing and fulfilling his Father's plan. When Jesus cries out, 'It is finished' (v. 30), he isn't simply saying that his own suffering is over and done with. He is declaring that his crucifixion is a finished work. Nothing more can be added to it. The debt has been paid.

I used to do some voluntary chaplaincy work in Brixton prison, London when it was a remand prison. It was a really eye-opening experience. Just to state the obvious, prison isn't a very nice place! You share a cell and a loo with a stranger. You are locked up for hours at a time, and your social life is intimately connected to a lot of people who have done terrible things. I vividly remember one man breaking down in tears as he was brought in for the first time and it dawned on him that this was his new home. As it was a remand prison, many of the inmates in Brixton were waiting for their trial or sentence. Understandably, the anticipation consumed them; they were all deeply preoccupied with what was going to happen. Would they be condemned? How would they be sentenced? How long would they stay here? They lived with permanent insecurity.

If we find ourself feeling insecure as a leader, it may be that we are experiencing ministry in the same way that the prisoners experienced life in Brixton prison; we are living our life on remand. We live with a lingering sense of condemnation, and a simmering anxiety about our future trial before the living God. The gospel of mercy has somehow faded into the background, leaving us empty and dry. Why else do we walk around with a vague sense of having to prove ourselves? Why else might we have a lingering feeling of self-condemnation and inadequacy? It is all too easy for leaders to live under a sense of unlimited obligation and with a feeling that they never measure up.

This is compounded by the inconsistencies, disobedience and spiritual mess in our lives. We feel our failures often, and at times very acutely, making us feel spiritually haunted. So, what will we do with this failure? How will we cope with burdened consciences and the sense that we don't measure up to our own standards, let alone God's? The answer is found at the finished work of the cross.

We are called to do for ourselves exactly what we are always asking other people to do: namely, to keep coming back to the good news of Jesus' finished work. We are called to live in the profound security of our debt having been paid. A few years ago, I was given the opportunity by the Student Loan Company to pay off the whole of my outstanding student loan at a reduced sum. I jumped at the opportunity and paid it off. However, when I received no notification in the post, I chased them, worrying that the money I'd transferred had disappeared somewhere. Happily, they did confirm that it was indeed paid off, and sent me my letter of confirmation. Jesus' declaration at the cross – 'It is finished' (v. 30) – is our letter of confirmation that the debt of all our sin has been paid off. The Son has spoken from his pulpit – the cross – and his short sermon answers every uncertainty we might have.

The effects of Jesus' death doubly underline this declaration in verse 30:

> Instead, one of the soldiers pierced Jesus' side with a spear, bringing a sudden flow of blood and water. The man who saw it has given testimony, and his testimony is true. He knows that he tells the truth, and he testifies so that you also may believe (vv. 34–35).

Blood and water plainly flow from Jesus' side. On one level, this simply tells us that his death was very real, and not imaginary. However, the deeper meaning here, as is often the case in John's Gospel, is in the allusion to spiritual realities. First of all, it is the blood of sacrifice. The Passover lamb has been sacrificed, fulfilling John's words in 1:29: 'The next day John saw Jesus coming towards him and said, "Look, the Lamb of God, who takes away the sin of the world!"' Jesus sheds his blood as his life is given up in violent sacrifice. While the blood of lambs and bulls could never take away sin, there is enough power in one drop of Jesus' blood to deal with the sins of thousands of worlds.[3]

In addition to the blood of sacrifice, John is alluding to the 'living water', already mentioned in John 7:37–38:

> On the last and greatest day of the festival, Jesus stood and said in a loud voice, 'Let anyone who is thirsty come to me and drink. Whoever believes in me, as Scripture has said, rivers of living water will flow from within them.

Jesus is bringing new life in the Spirit (v. 39). God's river of life is flowing into us, fulfilling the promise of Ezekiel 47:1–12. In summary, the cross is securing for us everything we could ever need – propitiation for and expiation of sin, and vast, immeasurable, ever-flowing life. This is the finished work of the cross for every disciple – and every leader.

John 19 therefore tells us that we're not called to fix ourselves, our church, our Bible study group or our family, because we can't. That's Jesus' job. He's the Rescuer, not us. We're not calling people to sort themselves out, however broken they might be. Only Jesus can fix the unfixable. The power for a changed relationship with God is in the royal crucifixion alone. It can't be replaced by steps, a programme, a course or my wise counsel. John 19 tell us that Christ crucified is the answer. He has paid the debt, his blood has been shed and he has poured out the water of life.

Power and leadership

As I write this, it has been a season in which a whole number of well-known church leaders have been accused of domineering, bullying and abusive behaviour. Different leaders have been exposed in their treatment of colleagues, congregation members and even family. A number of them have been removed from their roles. There is, accordingly, much debate about this issue. It's clear that, in some contexts, there have been awful mistreatment and toxic patterns of behaviour. As I've reflected on this, it has struck me that, while we wouldn't tolerate sexual immorality or serious doctrinal error in leaders, misuse of power is something of a blind spot. We have just not thought through how the way we exercise power relates to godly character.

What is surprising, though, is how we might miss this issue, given that we believe in a Saviour who died in weakness on a cross. As people who really believe in the finished work of Christ, how could we think that misuse of power is relatively unimportant when it comes to discipleship and leadership? The answer is complex and has to do with many things. Yet, there is an issue here with how we relate to the cross. The truth is that while we grasp the doctrine of the cross – we know about atonement, substitution and propitiation – on the other hand, we have failed to see what is right before our eyes: Jesus was *crucified*. We understand what Jesus achieved at the cross, but we need to grasp the actual nature of the cross as well. The doctrine easily becomes abstracted from the actual historical reality of crucifixion.

Crucifixion

In the summer of 1998, Westminster Abbey unveiled ten new statues over its main entrance. All the new statues are twentieth-century martyrs. They include a range of believers, such as Dietrich Bonhoeffer, Martin Luther King, Janani Luwum and Oscar Romero, who have died for their faith in some way. The statues obviously celebrate the lives of these remarkable people, yet they give no hint of *how* they died. The point is simply that they died. This is, in many ways, understandable – it would have been pretty macabre for the artists to have followed through with a depiction of their various methods of execution. That isn't what the average person on the street wants to see!

In contrast, what makes the Gospels so utterly different to anything else we know is what they choose to highlight. The accounts of Jesus' death make clear that he is not simply one more martyr for the faith. Their big focus is not Jesus' heroism, but the very manner of his death. *How* he died is actually key to their message. Let's not forget what is blindingly obvious but easily missed: Jesus isn't simply killed or murdered for sins; he is *crucified*. Look at how this is repeatedly mentioned and pointed out for us throughout John 19. We mustn't ignore it or sideline it, as my emphasis shows:

> As soon as the chief priests and their officials saw him, they shouted, '*Crucify! Crucify!*'
>
> But Pilate answered, 'You take him and *crucify* him' (v. 6).

> 'Do you refuse to speak to me?' Pilate said. 'Don't you realise I have power either to free you or to *crucify* you?' (v. 10).

> But they shouted, 'Take him away! Take him away! *Crucify* him!'
>
> 'Shall I *crucify* your king?' Pilate asked (v. 15).

> Finally Pilate handed him over to them to be *crucified* (v. 16).

> There they *crucified* him, and with him two others – one on each side and Jesus in the middle (v. 18).

> Many of the Jews read this sign, for the place where Jesus was *crucified* was near the city (v. 20).

> When the soldiers *crucified* Jesus, they took his clothes (v. 23).

The manner of Jesus' death is key. It's at the heart of the whole Gospel account, and central to the meaning of it.

For people in the ancient world, the cross wasn't just an instrument of execution, but the Roman Empire's way of showing its utter power and control over its population. It was symbolic of the tyrannical rule the authorities had over rebels. The very way that crucifixion killed people made this clear. For example, contrast crucifixion with modern capital punishment. Whatever we think of capital punishment, the modern-day electric chair is designed to be 'humane' and 'quick'. It uses a hood to veil the victim and is carried out indoors, away from public view. Crucifixion, on the other hand, was designed precisely to be protracted (over several days) and excruciating. On a Roman cross was a little step, which partially supported the weight of the victim. This wasn't a mercy, but was meant to prolong the slow asphyxiation of the victim by encouraging them to push up as they hung, gasping for air. Crucifixion was also designed to be public and humiliating. It was a public spectacle of utter degradation and shame before the power of Rome, serving as a terrifying warning for anyone who would dare rebel. The jeering crowds were part of the gruesome entertainment. In summary, crucifixion was intended not just to kill the victim, but to turn them into a non-entity. The sufferer was denied their common humanity. They were considered nothing more than human garbage and, in essence, eliminated as a member of the human race. Commonly, the victim was put on display stripped naked for all to see.

I remember showing my five-year-old daughter an animated Easter video, which included a brief depiction of the crucifixion. As any five-year-old might say, she exclaimed, 'I can see his pants.' I was initially annoyed at her observation and that she was obviously missing the point of what she was seeing! However, something then dawned on me: the filmmaker was very happy to depict the crucifixion, but, at the same time, they obviously felt a need to put underwear on Jesus. Why? Most likely, because we would all be embarrassed by seeing him naked on the cross. It would seem disrespectful. We want to 'protect' Jesus and not expose him to shame. We feel a need to put fig leaves on his crucified naked body. The shame of the cross is hard for us to bear.

Royal crucifixion

Given the horror and degradation of crucifixions, we can see why it was so completely shocking that the first believers didn't try to hide Jesus' death on the cross. For any person in the ancient world, crucifixion was disturbing. You would have expected that the early Christians would have wanted to sideline, obscure or even deny it. One can hardly think of anything more unsuitable as the source of hope and faith. Yet, for the first Christians, Jesus' crucifixion was the centre of their preaching and rejoicing. Two thousand years later, it's impossible to conceive of Christianity in any other terms. While Imperial Rome had imposed a particular meaning on crucifixion, this was, incredibly, subverted as the early believers rejoiced in the scandal and stigma of Jesus' death:

> Therefore let all Israel be assured of this: God has made this Jesus, whom you crucified, both Lord and Messiah (Acts 2:36).

> I have been crucified with Christ and I no longer live, but Christ lives in me. The life I now live in the body, I live by faith in the Son of God, who loved me and gave himself for me (Gal. 2:20).

> May I never boast except in the *cross* of our Lord Jesus Christ (Gal. 6:14, my emphasis).

John 19 is part of this subversive retelling of Jesus' death, but makes the point that this is a *royal* crucifixion. Jesus declares earlier in John's Gospel that:

> The hour has come for the Son of Man to be glorified (12:23).

> Now the Son of Man is glorified and God is glorified in him (13:31).

The cross is where Jesus' royal glory will be put on display, as he loves those he has come to save by dying for them. In chapters 18–19, we see Jesus debating with Pilate about his kingdom. Funnily enough, throughout the interrogation, Pilate serves as God's prophet, unwittingly proclaiming the good news that Jesus is the King:

- Jesus is forced to wear a crown – of thorns (19:2).
- Pilate calls Jesus 'king' (v. 14).

- A sign is made for the cross, in three languages, declaring Jesus to be king (v. 19).

In other words, Pilate's malice serves God's purpose in proclaiming Jesus as God's King.

If we fast-forward to the burial of Jesus in verses 38–42, we see the royal theme continuing. Normally, crucifixion victims were left on crosses to rot and be eaten by vultures, or thrown onto a special burial site for criminals outside Jerusalem.[4] As we've seen, Rome intended crucifixion to erase someone from the human race, and the Jewish leaders would have wanted Jesus dishonoured and removed. Yet, two friends – Joseph and Nicodemus – risk themselves for Jesus. While Peter had denied knowing Jesus, and the other disciples had ran way, these two unknown disciples align themselves with their King (even if they are quaking at the knees, v. 38). They use their connections to collect Jesus' body and give him a royal burial. Jesus' body isn't destined to be left to rot on the cross nor thrown on an unclean burial site, but is to be buried in a rich man's tomb. The amount of burial spices brought to anoint Jesus' body in verse 39 is also striking. It is actually a massive amount, enough for a king (see also 12:7). While the soldiers, who take charge of Jesus, stripped him and crucified him as a piece of trash, Jesus is now honoured, clothed and given lavish royal treatment.

Notice, then, how the majesty of Christ is at work in the midst of shame and humiliation. The crucifixion of

Jesus brings together opposites that would seem otherwise impossible to reconcile. Life is at work in death. Power is at work in weakness. Sovereignty is at work in catastrophe. Jesus rules even as he suffers. Amazingly, the crucifixion isn't a denial of his kingship, but a revelation of it. The cross is Jesus' throne, and this is beyond what anyone might naturally have conceived. No one could ever invent this.

The implications for leaders, who steward power on behalf of the risen Christ, are massive. No leader who believes in such a Saviour can ever lead the same way again. The humiliation and degradation of his crucifixion transforms all ministry. All lust for power and control has been crucified with Jesus. Domination, manipulation and aggression can no longer characterise our relationships – as these are the very things that crucified our Lord. Human jockeying for position, power and influence look ridiculous alongside such a suffering King.

Thus, we should take a good look at ourselves in light of the cross before it's too late. A cross-shaped ministry isn't simply a ministry that preaches the right truths about Jesus' death, but is a ministry that lives out his death in the very way it operates. Atonement theology can't be a substitute for cross-centred living. If we find ourselves tempted to be controlling, overbearing and too pushy, we should refresh our knowledge of the crucified Saviour. If we find ourselves jockeying for power, looking for influence and seeking to promote ourselves, we need to go back to the cross to find out what true glory is. We don't want our ministries to look more like Imperial Rome than the King of kings. We need to know the crucified King if we are to live out a pattern of ministry that will faithfully emulate him.

– 9 –

Seeing Jesus

Early on the first day of the week, while it was still dark, Mary Magdalene went to the tomb and saw that the stone had been removed from the entrance. So she came running to Simon Peter and the other disciple, the one Jesus loved, and said, 'They have taken the Lord out of the tomb, and we don't know where they have put him!'

So Peter and the other disciple started for the tomb. Both were running, but the other disciple outran Peter and reached the tomb first. He bent over and looked in at the strips of linen lying there but did not go in. Then Simon Peter came along behind him and went straight into the tomb. He saw the strips of linen lying there, as well as the cloth that had been wrapped round Jesus' head. The cloth was still lying in its place, separate from the linen. Finally the other disciple, who had reached the tomb first, also went inside. He saw and believed. (They still did not understand from Scripture that Jesus had to rise from the dead.) Then the disciples went back to where they were staying.

Now Mary stood outside the tomb crying. As she wept, she bent over to look into the tomb and saw two angels in white, seated where Jesus' body had been, one at the head and the other at the foot.

They asked her, 'Woman, why are you crying?'

'They have taken my Lord away,' she said, 'and I don't know where they have put him.' At this, she turned round and saw Jesus standing there, but she did not realise that it was Jesus.

He asked her, 'Woman, why are you crying? Who is it you are looking for?'

Thinking he was the gardener, she said, 'Sir, if you have carried him away, tell me where you have put him, and I will get him.'

Jesus said to her, 'Mary.'

She turned towards him and cried out in Aramaic, 'Rabboni!' (which means 'Teacher').

Jesus said, 'Do not hold on to me, for I have not yet ascended to the Father. Go instead to my brothers and tell them, "I am ascending to my Father and your Father, to my God and your God."'

Mary Magdalene went to the disciples with the news: 'I have seen the Lord!' And she told them that he had said these things to her.

On the evening of that first day of the week, when the disciples were together, with the doors locked for fear of the Jewish leaders, Jesus came and stood among them and said, 'Peace be with you!' After he said this, he showed them his hands and side. The disciples were overjoyed when they saw the Lord.

Again Jesus said, 'Peace be with you! As the Father has sent me, I am sending you.' And with that he breathed on them and said, 'Receive the Holy Spirit. If you forgive anyone's sins, their sins are forgiven; if you do not forgive them, they are not forgiven.'

Now Thomas (also known as Didymus), one of the Twelve, was not with the disciples when Jesus came. So the other disciples told him, 'We have seen the Lord!'

But he said to them, 'Unless I see the nail marks in his hands and put my finger where the nails were, and put my hand into his side, I will not believe.'

A week later his disciples were in the house again, and Thomas was with them. Though

> the doors were locked, Jesus came and stood among them and said, 'Peace be with you!' Then he said to Thomas, 'Put your finger here; see my hands. Reach out your hand and put it into my side. Stop doubting and believe.'
>
> Thomas said to him, 'My Lord and my God!'
>
> Then Jesus told him, 'Because you have seen me, you have believed; blessed are those who have not seen and yet have believed.'
>
> Jesus performed many other signs in the presence of his disciples, which are not recorded in this book. But these are written that you may believe that Jesus is the Messiah, the Son of God, and that by believing you may have life in his name (John 20:1–31).

When you think about it, it is surprising that the Great Pyramid of Giza, built around 2500 BC, is one of the greatest tourist destinations of the world. It's an ancient grave in a desolate desert in the Middle East, but it's officially one of the seven wonders of the ancient world and draws over fourteen million visitors each year. The pyramids are the most famous graves in the world and have enduring global iconic status. The world is full of other famous burial places, such as Mohammed's tomb, Elvis Presley's grave in Memphis and the Taj Mahal mausoleum, built as a memorial to a wife of one of India's Shahs. In the UK, Westminster Abbey is the resting place for the bodies of long-dead

English nobles and notables. All these burial places draw visitors and tourists from across the world. However, there is one famous grave that is very different: the tomb of Jesus. His tomb is famous not because it has something in it, but because there is nothing inside. It is an empty tomb. In fact, so empty was his tomb that its true location is lost in time, and is only the subject of conjecture today. One might wonder why Jesus' followers didn't make greater efforts to preserve his grave. The answer is obvious once you know the gospel: the first believers weren't interested in marking the spot where Jesus had been buried because Jesus wasn't there anymore! His tomb had been emptied. He had risen from the dead.

If our ministry is going to be a Christian ministry, it has to be based on an empty tomb and a risen Jesus. Resurrection is the substance of what we are about – or our preaching isn't good news according to the apostles:

> And if Christ has not been raised, our preaching is useless and so is your faith. More than that, we are then found to be false witnesses about God, for we have testified about God that he raised Christ from the dead ... If only for this life we have hope in Christ, we are of all people most to be pitied (1 Cor. 15:14–15, 19).

We live by faith in the risen Lord and live now as witnesses to him. Ministry, by the power of the Holy Spirit, is about waking the world up to the enormity of what happened in the tomb of Jesus two thousand years ago. We're not calling people to come on pilgrimage to the grave of a long-dead Rabbi, but are heralding the resurrected Lord.

Seeing the resurrection

Before the coronavirus pandemic hit the world in spring 2020, many failed to really grasp what was going on. Leaders and politicians across the board failed to see its implications. The most significant thing in our lifetimes was happening right in front of our eyes, but we didn't get it. Over time, our eyes were forced open to the reality of it all and we understood. Much the same could be said of the disciples as they experienced the resurrection. Here was a history-changing, global event, but it wasn't clear to the apostles what had just happened. They needed to have their eyes opened to what was going on.

John 20 serves to open our eyes to Jesus. It mentions 'seeing' numerous times (for example, vv. 1, 6, 8, 12, 25, 27). The disciples can see physically, but the question is whether or not they have eyes to see spiritual reality. In the first part of the chapter, the picture seems pretty discouraging. The disciples seem to fail to get what is going on, or they understand something of the truth but don't grasp it by faith. Resurrection might be all around you, but you could still fail to comprehend it.

Seeing the empty tomb

As we have already seen, on Good Friday, Joseph and Nicodemus had given Jesus a royal funeral (19:38–42). They had lavished spices on him fit for a king and carefully wrapped him in strips of linen. With honour and respect, they had placed his body in Joseph's family tomb before the Sabbath. On the first day of the week, Mary now goes to the tomb to help prepare Jesus' body. Dramatically, though, the body isn't there. Mary sees that the tomb has already been opened and draws the obvious conclusion: the body has been stolen. She declares, 'They have taken the Lord out of the tomb' (20:13), though it's unclear exactly who the 'they' are meant to be – Roman soldiers? Chief priests? Grave robbers? In her mind, however, the body has definitely been stolen.

In response to what Mary tells them, Peter and John ('the other disciple', v. 3) immediately run to the tomb.[1] They have been absent from the story since Peter's denial of Jesus, but now they are eager to know what has happened. When they get there, Peter 'sees' strips of linen, neatly folded up (vv. 6–7), and John goes in and 'sees' the empty tomb (v. 8). Verse 8 also tells us that John 'saw and believed', yet in verse 9 we're told they still didn't really understand what was going on. Again, they lack spiritual insight. Their anti-climactic walk home is further evidence of their confusion. Tellingly, they don't linger as Mary does. The disciples see the empty tomb, and the strips of linen, but they clearly haven't yet come to full faith.[2] They still don't have spiritual understanding of the Scriptures and Jesus' resurrection. We're reminded that seeing with our eyes isn't the same as seeing with the fulness of faith.

Seeing the risen Jesus

The disciples leave Jesus' tomb, but Mary stays. She is crying, overwhelmed and feeling abandoned. She had witnessed the gruesome torture and death of her Lord, and now feels a deep sense of God's absence. Yet ironically, as she weeps, she is stood right next to where Jesus has just risen from the dead! There is a sense in which she too is full of spiritual blindness (which is alluded to with the words 'it was still dark', v. 1).[3] She sees the empty tomb (v. 11), two angels (v. 12) and even Jesus himself (v. 14), but fails to 'get it' every time. She even complains to the angels about the missing body and mistakes her risen Lord as someone there for mere horticultural duties (v. 13). She calls Jesus 'Lord' (v. 13), but is really only looking for a corpse. In the irony of ironies, she addresses Jesus wondering if he has stolen his own body (v. 15)! We learn here that you can have the empty tomb, angels and the risen Jesus himself stood right in front of you, but not understand.

Strikingly, the most significant, visible and dramatic of all the signs in John's Gospel does not immediately elicit faith. This confirms that faith is more than simply responding to the empirical evidence before us. Physical sight and signs aren't actually sufficient for a robust faith. Conversion needs more than an assessment of the evidence and the cogent presentation of arguments. We might be tempted to think that if only God could send somebody a sign, then they would believe. We might hope that powerful encounters and dramatic interventions will deliver people from unbelief and vindicate our message. Yet, John 20 reminds us that signs and wonders won't automatically remove unbelief. The risen Jesus appearing at the bottom of someone's bed won't just sort everything out.

What is needed is God's intervention to grant spiritual insight and understanding. Lack of empirical evidence isn't the real problem in conversion. Rather, the obstacle is the human heart and a mind that is fallen and unable to 'see' spiritual realities. So, don't be discouraged in your ministry by thinking that what you're really lacking is some kind of spiritual magic to compel people to believe. The human heart is hard even in the face of incredible evidence to the contrary.

What changes the situation for Mary isn't the appearance of Jesus in front of her, but his word to her in verse 16. Notice that when Jesus comes to Mary, he doesn't do some wonder to convince her that he has come back. On the contrary, he simply speaks her name. Yet, this isn't just a repetition of her name; it is a summons to faith. In the same way that Jesus summoned Lazarus from the grave (11:43–44), or that the Shepherd knows the sheep by name and they know his voice (10:3, 16), so Jesus is summoning Mary out of the darkness and into the light. He is opening her blind eyes. This is the miracle of new birth that enables someone to believe in the miracle of the resurrection. This is what will change our unbelieving friends. We can't do this ourselves – only the Lord can summon them out of darkness with his word.

Mary is clearly transformed as she encounters Jesus. With her eyes opened to the truth, there is new-found joy. Yet, even here, she's still learning who Jesus is. She grabs hold of him, but Jesus won't let her treat him like a private dream-come-true. The Jesus before her is far bigger and more powerful than what she bargained for:

> Do not hold on to me, for I have not yet returned to the Father. Go instead to my brothers and tell them, 'I am returning to my Father and your Father, to my God and your God' (20:17).

Mary wants to hold onto Jesus as her private possession, but he won't let her keep him for herself. He is the risen Lord and she is now under his command. Accordingly, she is sent out to share the good news with others. Whereas in verses 1–2 she saw the tomb and said that someone had stolen Jesus' body, in verse 18 her message is, 'I have seen the Lord!' The result of her eyes being opened is witness to the world. Powerful personal experiences always have a centrifugal effect – they send us out to share the gospel with others. Excitement and joy naturally overflow into evangelism. A powerful encounter with Jesus necessarily leads to proclamation of Jesus to others. Our delight in him means we can't just keep him for ourselves. This is exactly what is about to happen to the disciples.

The risen Jesus appears

This, then, is the unexpected background for the appearances of the risen Jesus to the disciples themselves. They hear the good news of his resurrection from Mary, but it's unclear how it has affected them. As verse 19 begins, it seems that they were continuing to live as disciples without the hope of resurrection. This was no bold band of brothers, but shaking 'scaredy-cats' cowering behind locked doors as they trembled before the Jewish leaders. These weren't the courageous men we see later, but terrified and confused disciples.

They have, though, two big encounters with the risen Jesus, and each is decisive and transformative. Notice that in both encounters, Jesus comes how and when he wishes, without invitation or request. There are no locked doors for him. And when he appears as promised, he comes with incredible blessing, mercy and love.

Firstly, he speaks peace over them, on three occasions (vv. 19, 21, 26). He had already promised them his peace during his final speech before the cross: 'Peace I leave with you; my peace I give you. I do not give to you as the world gives. Do not let your hearts be troubled and do not be afraid' (14:27). Now he brings them that peace: 'Jesus came and stood among them and said, "Peace be with you!"' (20:19). We should remember that peace in the Bible is heavenly life, not just some calm feeling that we have inside of us. This life is wellness with no qualifications and the fulness of flourishing. Peace, biblically speaking, is the world restored, put back together and filled with the presence of God. As the risen High Priest, Jesus speaks Aaron's blessing over his people (cf. Num. 6:22–27).

Secondly, in both appearances, Jesus shows the disciples his hands and his side (vv. 20, 27). This seems a strange thing to do. After all, if they needed to recognise him, couldn't they just look at his face?! But Jesus' aim here is redemption, not recognition. These wounds are his credentials – the sign of a fulfilled and finished work (19:30). The resurrection hasn't obliterated his scars and wounds, despite a new glorified body, because the marks of his suffering are part of his glory. His suffering on the cross isn't something to move on from, like some bad experience or a nightmare from the past, but is to be remembered eternally. The marks are permanent because our salvation is permanent. The words of the prophet Isaiah have a peculiar resonance in light of this:

> Can a mother forget the baby at her breast
> and have no compassion on the child she has borne?
> Though she may forget,
> I will not forget you!
> See, I have engraved you on the palms of my hands ... (Isa. 49:15–16).

Being engraved on the palms of the Son of God means that the risen Prince of Peace is also our Crucified King.

Thirdly, the disciples are transformed. Fear becomes joy in verse 20, fulfilling Jesus' earlier prediction: 'So with you: now is your time of grief, but I will see you again and you will rejoice, and no one will take away your joy' (16:22). Yet, the disciples, like Mary, aren't allowed to enjoy the risen Jesus as some private, personal experience. The endpoint isn't simply that they will know that Jesus is risen, or even that they will be filled with joy. Rather, like Mary, the disciples are being sent out to share that good news with others. Jesus' resurrection immediately drives them out in witness to the world: 'As the Father has sent me, I am sending you' (20:21). The resurrection isn't a personal comfort, but a message to be made known. And, as leaders, we've been thrust and pushed out by the Lord Jesus into the world to make him known. Notice how Jesus doesn't ask the disciples for their permission before sending them out, any more than he asks for their permission to appear! The Lord doesn't try to persuade, nor does he give a rousing motivational speech. In fact, he doesn't even wait for acceptance and agreement. He just states facts: 'I am sending you.' The question concerning us is not whether or not we've been sent out, but how we can now go about this business of making Jesus known.

Do you feel reluctant about that mission? Leaders can be 'scaredy-cats' as much as the disciples were. We are as prone to fear and worry about how we'll be received. Yet, if we do find ourselves preferring to hide quietly behind some locked doors, then we should look at verses 22–23. We see there that Jesus gives the disciples his Spirit, and then he gives them authority to preach the gospel. They start dispirited, but now become Spirit-filled men through the risen Jesus. So, he doesn't just send them out, but empowers them for ministry and grants them his authority. Verse 23 also tells us that the forgiveness of people's sins will depend on the message the disciples, and now we, preach. We're not empty and alone in our work, but empowered and authorised. We step out not in timidity, but with good news of the forgiveness of God for sin. This hope means that we really can unlock the doors and go out in the strength of the risen Christ.

Seeing is believing?

The second appearance of Jesus to the disciples has a lot of similarities to the first. Again, it happens on the first day of the week, and in the same house. Again, the doors are locked, and the same greeting of peace is given. However, the circumstances are different. The focus now is on one famous disciple, Thomas. The issue this time isn't so much fear, but sheer unbelief. We don't know why Thomas wasn't there the first time around, but we do know that he'd heard the gospel of the resurrection. He had received the same witness that the disciples had received from Mary (v. 18), and had also received the apostles' testimony, 'We have seen the Lord' (v. 25).

Thomas has missed out not on hearing the gospel, but on seeing the risen Jesus. His response to this is a demand, or a condition: he will only believe if he can see and touch. At best, Thomas seems to envisage faith as a kind of negotiation with Jesus. At worst, this is a very bold, and spiritually dangerous, declaration of unbelief in the risen Lord. At any rate, Thomas isn't unlike others in the Gospel of John who demand signs if they are to have faith (see, for example, 6:30).

The surprising thing here, though, is how Jesus actually seems to listen to Thomas' demands. Jesus obviously heard his disciples, even when he wasn't physically with them, and he knew their doubts and fears (and unbelief). Jesus appears to actually indulge Thomas in some sense. He doesn't excommunicate him from the Twelve, but comes to him with tremendous mercy and pastoral patience. He is gentle, even as he authoritatively summons Thomas out of darkness and opens his blind eyes. Notice all the commands in verse 27: 'put', 'see', 'reach', 'put', 'stop doubting', 'believe'. Thomas is being rescued here from himself. The biggest irony of the whole of John 20 comes in verse 28, as the unbelieving disciple ends up making one of the strongest and clearest statements about who Jesus is in the whole of the New Testament: 'My Lord and my God'! The faithless apostle becomes the brilliant faith-filled preacher.

Yet, if we're honest, we're left with a lingering question for ourselves: 'How will we believe?' We might, in reading this, feel a bit left out like Thomas. While we might not expect Jesus to turn up in our living room, wouldn't it be nice to have a bit more reassurance that he is real and alive and with us?! Jesus answers this for us when correcting Thomas: 'Because you have seen me, you have believed; blessed are those who have not seen and yet have believed' (v. 29). We have read a lot about 'seeing' in this story. It seems, as we look back over it, that it isn't wrong per se to have our faith strengthened from what we see. After all, Jesus did perform visible signs and wonders all through his ministry, as the Gospel of John testifies. Further, the disciples have *seen* the empty tomb and Jesus has just *appeared* to them several times. Yet, Jesus teaches us in verse 29 that living faith is built on God's word, not signs and wonders. 'Blessed', in other words, are those whose faith is grounded in God's word alone – and not in anything they can see or touch. Back in verses 8–9, we read of how the disciples saw and believed in some way, but didn't understand the Scripture. What we can infer from this is that faith is meant to build on Scripture, not on what we see. Verses 30–31 confirm this:

> Jesus performed many other signs in the presence of his disciples, which are not recorded in this book. But these are written that you may believe that Jesus is the Messiah, the Son of God, and that by believing you may have life in his name.

John says that he has written all the things in his Gospel so that we may know and believe in Jesus. In other words, we may not see Jesus or his miracles, but we can know Jesus and his miracles through what is 'written'. We don't need to have touched his side or his hands; we can get 'life' through what is written down. We haven't missed out, nor have we been sidelined, nor have we been sent to the back of the queue. On the contrary, we have been given the word of God! This will be enough for us.

Back in verse 29, Jesus actually says that we who believe on the basis of this word are 'blessed': 'Because you have seen me, you have believed; blessed are those who have not seen and yet have believed.' That might seem very strange because, to all intents and purposes, it looks like the disciples were the blessed ones. This is exactly how many of the people that we lead think. Their Christian life feels like a derivative, hand-me-down, second-hand blessing. They can feel a bit sidelined, as if they've missed out on something. A word-centred faith can seem to lack sparkle and pizzazz. It's almost a bit boring as we don't see that much.

However, Jesus is saying here that if we believe the word about him, then we actually receive a blessing that Thomas himself didn't get. This is really quite remarkable. When the risen Lord Jesus is standing in front of the disciples, he says that the real blessing is for others who aren't in the room! We receive a blessing, through faith in the risen Jesus, that the apostles did not receive! Our congregations, Bible studies and student groups aren't full of second-class citizens with a second-class blessing. The risen Jesus is all ours today and smiles over our little lives.

Be encouraged that, as you fight the fight of ministry, you do not do this alone, or dependent upon your own resources. On the contrary, you live in the presence of the risen Lord Jesus himself and, by faith in him, you have inherited a blessing greater even than that given to the apostles. Just as the people you lead aren't second-class citizens in the kingdom, nor are you a second-class leader. Jesus is alive, and as you follow him, you have all you need in the gospel.

Notes

1. Following Jesus

1. C. S. Lewis, *Voyage to Venus* (Pan Books, 1953), p. 14.
2. Though Luke and John are different Gospels with different authors and different intentions, they have the same ultimate Author. There are no accidents or coincidences in inspired Scripture.
3. C. S. Lewis, *The Horse and His Boy* in *The Chronicles of Narnia* (Collins, 2001), p. 299.

2. Loving Jesus

1. John Newton, *Additional Letters* (2013), Kindle edition, location 204.
2. Ibid., location 1463.
3. The Greek word that is used many places in the Gospels, when talking about Jesus' love for us, is *splanchnizō*. It can be translated 'to have compassion' or 'to have pity'. It describes Jesus' great love going out to people. The word is actually connected to the bowels and so gives us a vivid description of how Jesus is physically moved in his compassion for lost and broken people, like us.
4. Taken from Charles H. Spurgeon, 'The love of Jesus, what it is – none but his loved ones know' (Metropolitan Tabernacle Pulpit, volume 8, 18 June 1862).
5. Just to be clear, I'm not suggesting that people struggling with such issues are more lost than the self-righteous middle classes. Pharisees and demoniacs are equally lost. My point is simply that the effects of sin get an extreme depiction in these circumstances.

3. Depending on Jesus

1. See Mark 5:26. Luke, the doctor, seems to have omitted this detail in his Gospel!
2. John Newton, *The Letters of John Newton* (Monergism Books, 2011), Kindle edition, location 21758.
3. Paul E. Miller, *A Praying Life* (NavPress, 2009), p. 119.
4. J. C. Ryle, *Light from Old Times* (LightByDesign.net), Kindle edition, location 2525.
5. John Newton, *The Letters of John Newton* (Monergism Books, 2011), Kindle edition, location 316.

4. Feeding on Jesus

1. I'm indebted to Tim Keller for this point (see https://www.thegospelcoalition.org/article/3-ways-ministry-can-make-you-conceited/).
2. John Calvin, *The Institutes of the Christian Religion*, 2.16.19 (Westminster Press, 2016), p. 527.

5. Proclaiming Jesus

1. Andrew Murray, *Humility* (Wilder Publications, 2008), Kindle edition, location 119.
2. Craig S. Keener, *The Gospel of John: A Commentary* (Baker Academic, 2003), p. 448.

6. Slaving for Jesus

1. For an overview, see Collin Hansen (ed.), *Our Secular Age* (The Gospel Coalition, 2017), Kindle edition.
2. I am indebted in this chapter to Murray J. Harris, *Slave of Christ* (Apollos, 1999) for some basic insights into the New Testament and slavery.
3. The 2011 text of the NIV Bible uses 'slave'.
4. See Dane Ortlund, *Gentle and Lowly* (Crossway, 2020) for his well-known exposition of these verses.

7. Longing for Jesus

1. In the original Greek, the word 'long' in Luke 17:22 is strong – it can mean to covet or lust for something.
2. J. C. Ryle, *Expository Thoughts on the Gospels*, Volumes 1–4, Kindle edition, location 16367.

8. Knowing Jesus

1. Quoted in Fleming Rutledge, *The Crucifixion* (William B. Eerdmans, 2015), p. 115.
2. The original Greek words are slightly different in verse 28 but overlap significantly in meaning.
3. Charles H. Spurgeon, *A Defence of Calvinism* (Banner of Truth, 2010), p. 20. His comment is based on John Owen: 'There is enough grace, mercy and pardon in one of God's promises for the sins of millions of worlds, if they existed, because the promise is supplied from an infinite, bottomless reservoir.' See John Owen, *Communion with God* (Banner of Truth, 1991), p. 62.
4. Craig S. Keener, *The Gospel of John: A Commentary* (Baker Academic, 2003), pp. 1157–1158.

9. Seeing Jesus

1. Running was a culturally undignified thing to do, so shows their urgency.
2. John's Gospel had made clear before that even though it looks like someone 'believes', the true nature of their faith can be ambiguous (see, for example, John 2:23–24). That ambiguity of 'belief' is present in this passage too.
3. Having said this, we shouldn't be too hard on Mary as she is clearly very loyal to Jesus, and remained faithful to him when others had fled.

10 Publishing
a division of 10 of those.com

10Publishing is the publishing house of **10ofThose**. It is committed to producing quality Christian resources that are biblical and accessible.

www.10ofthose.com is our online retail arm selling thousands of quality books at discounted prices.

For information contact: **info@10ofthose.com**
or check out our website: **www.10ofthose.com**